The History of Communication

Robert W. McChesney and
John C. Nerone, editors

Books in the Series

Last Rights

Last Rights

Revisiting
Four Theories of the Press

❖ ❖ ❖

Edited by John C. Nerone

WRITTEN BY

William E. Berry

Sandra Braman

Clifford Christians

Thomas G. Guback

Steven J. Helle

Louis W. Liebovich

John C. Nerone

Kim B. Rotzoll

University of Illinois Press ❖ Urbana and Chicago

© 1995 by the Board of Trustees of the University of Illinois
Manufactured in the United States of America
1 2 3 4 5 C P 5 4 3 2 1

This book is printed on acid-free paper.

Library of Congress Cataloging-in-Publication Data

Last rights : revisiting four theories of the press / edited by John
  C. Nerone ; written by William E. Berry . . . et al.
      p.   cm. — (The History of communication)
  Includes bibliographical references and index.
  ISBN 0-252-02180-0 (alk. paper). — ISBN 0-252-06470-4 (pbk.)
  1. Press and politics. 2. Freedom of the press. 3. Journalistic
ethics. I. Nerone, John C. II. Berry, William E.   III. Series.
PN4751L37   1995
070'.01—dc20   95-3566
                                                          CIP

Contents

Preface

This book began a few years ago when Lou Liebovich and Jim Carey had the same idea at the same time. Both thought it would be a good idea for the communications faculty at Illinois to revisit that school's most famous product, the book *Four Theories of the Press*. *Four Theories* was conceived in Gregory Hall, where Illinois's College of Communications remains located; it was written by three men who each at one time headed the communications faculty; it has been used, either as text or whipping boy, by generations of Illinois faculty, and it remains the best-selling nonfiction book published by the University of Illinois Press. Carey, at the time the dean of the College of Communications, invited Cliff Christians to put together a task force to ponder the matter.

In our initial meetings, which Cliff chaired, the group determined that there were really two tasks at hand. The first was to assess the continuing relevance of *Four Theories* in a post–cold war world. The second was to erect a successor. We agreed that we had things to contribute to the first task—we all had made judgments on the map of normative press theory that *Four Theories* presents. There was less agreement on drawing a new map. So we decided to concentrate on critiquing and, for the time being, to limit remapping. (As we point out in the conclusion, many of us are already at work on new maps of this field.)

After we settled on a mission, we began to consider how we might accomplish it. First, we each drew up an abstract of the individual contributions we thought we might make. At that point, the group elected John Nerone to direct its proceedings and edit the final volume. Nerone developed an outline based on the individual abstracts and asked the group to decide on a format for the eventual book. After some serious disagreement, we decided to present the book as a report in one voice, much like the report of the Hutchins Commission. Each author would compose his or her pieces, and then Nerone would combine them to form a seamless text. To facilitate a rough equality of tone and prevent jarring inconsistencies among the parts, we circulated them—each author read every other author's material, then passed comments to Nerone, who fed them back to the authors, who used them in the process of revision. After all of the material had gone through this process, Nerone edited the parts into chapters and circulated the chapters to the authors for comment and criticism.

Every section of this book, then, passed through a long process of review, revision, editing, and more revision. In this sense, every section is collectively authored, but in another sense every section remains the contribution of a particular author. In each chapter, the introductory material is Nerone's. The rest was authored as follows: Chapter 1: "The Historical Moment of *Four Theories*" (Guback), "Theoretical Shortcomings" (Nerone), "Internal Inconsistencies and Inadequacies" (Guback and Nerone), "Silences and Absences" (Guback), "A Legacy Revisited" (Nerone); Chapter 2: "The Dilemma of Authoritarianism" (Nerone), "The Persistence of Authoritarianism" (Nerone), "The Libertarian Theory" (Nerone), "The Invention of a Marketplace of Ideas" (Nerone), "Libertarianism and Neoliberalism in First Amendment Law" (Helle), "Recent Innovations in Liberal Theory" (Christians), "Multiculturalism and Postmodernism" (Nerone); Chapter 3: "Responsibility, Yes; Theory, No?" (Liebovich), "The Radical Nature of Responsibility" (Christians), "William Ernest Hocking" (Christians), "Hocking's Intellectual Tradition" (Christians), "'Positive Freedom' as the 'Entering Wedge'"

(Helle), "Responsibility Endorses Liberalism" (Nerone), "Has the Press Become Responsible?" (Liebovich), "Will Technology Make Responsibility Obsolete?" (Berry), "Advertising as a Special Case" (Rotzoll), "Conclusion" (Nerone); Chapter 4: "Revisiting the Soviet Communist Theory of the Press" (Liebovich), "The Marxist Critique of Liberalism" (Guback), "Alternatives to Capitalism" (Guback); Chapter 5: "Globalization and the Decline of the Nation-State" (Braman), "The Decline of the Press" (Braman), "The Changing Relationship between the Press and the State" (Braman), "Public and Private" (Nerone); Conclusion (Nerone).

Our title is intentionally ambiguous. "Last rights" is an obvious pun on Last Rites, the sacrament of blessing at the point of death, and suggests not so much the demise of *Four Theories* as the end of the era that produced it. Contrarily, we also mean "last" in the sense of "to endure." Finally, "last rights" suggests a counterpoint to "first freedoms," a common title for works on freedom of speech and press.

The authors are grateful to more people than we can mention for making this book possible. First, we thank Jim Carey for bringing us together, and we forgive him for abandoning us when he moved to Columbia University. Ted Peterson, the surviving author of *Four Theories,* has been more than generous, reading much of the initial draft, sharing material he has written himself, and graciously tolerating our criticism of his earlier work. The complete manuscript was read and commented on by Kaarle Nordenstreng, whose suggestions and support were most helpful; by Bob McChesney, an invaluable colleague in these matters; and by Ted Glasser, who took hours from a busy schedule to give timely and generous advice. Richard Wentworth of the University of Illinois Press has been an eager supporter throughout the process. The manuscript also benefited from the attention of Theresa L. Sears and Margie Towery at the Press. Diane Tipps and Anita Specht have been indispensable.

Last Rights

1

Revisiting
Four Theories of the Press

❖ ❖ ❖

Why should we devote a book to *Four Theories of the Press?* Anyone would understand the appropriateness of writing a book about, say, Plato's *Republic* or Charles Darwin's *Origin of Species;* are we claiming that *Four Theories* deserves similar attention as one of the "great books" of Western civilization? Nothing would embarrass the authors of *Four Theories* more; they certainly have made no claims to transcendent achievement. Moreover, we are not in agreement about the intellectual merits of *Four Theories.*

We do agree that *Four Theories* has had a tremendous impact on teaching and thinking about freedom of the press. This impact is partly a result of superficial qualities. Some say that the book's popularity comes mainly from its brevity and simplicity. We can't deny the importance of these qualities in the book's success as a classroom teaching tool but we don't feel the book's appeal is limited to those qualities. Others have pointed out that the book fit elegantly into the agenda of the United States and its media during the cold war, an argument that is made at length later in this chapter. Again, while not denying this assessment, we still maintain that the book had and has other virtues.

Two chief virtues can be identified here. One is the curricular virtue of providing an alternative way of thinking about the press and society. A second is the intellectual virtue of outlining and beginning to grapple with some contradictions in classical liberalism that media scholars and practitioners had not yet really engaged. Let's turn first to curriculum.

The dominant way of thinking about normative press theory in the United States has been through law. The best-known books about "freedom of the press" in the past fifty years have been written by legal scholars or legal philosophers. These books, however, are often frustrating in subtle ways to those of us who think specifically about the media, because on the whole the great legal scholars subsume the media under the broader rubric of the First Amendment and freedom of expression (e.g., Emerson 1977; Dworkin 1977). Much of the work of the law that pertains to communication is not First Amendment law, but this broader terrain is treated only rarely by those interested in the press (Braman 1988). First Amendment scholars often do not distinguish the press—the institutional collectivity of news organizations—from other means of expression—speech, assembly, petition, worship. Moreover, within the U.S. tradition of liberal jurisprudence, they tend to understand their subject matter in terms of individuals rather than institutions. The rights of the press are implicitly assumed to be composed of individual rights or to be a means to the end of serving individual rights (e.g., Barron 1973). While this is not true of all legal scholarship, the exceptions are such that they tend not to come to the attention of undergraduate teachers of courses such as media law.

These tendencies of legal research have two results: first, they tend to make it difficult to discuss the operation of the press as an institution in society. Questions along these lines are continually translated into terms of individual cases, individual actors, and individual victims. Second, legal research encourages a manner of thinking and teaching that presents obstacles to certain normative discussions. On a practical level, legal thinking de-

mands great erudition in both theory and case history. Legal scholars resolve disputes by expanding the number and types of cases,
decisions, and pieces of legislation to be discussed. The expertise
required has meant that most people, and certainly most students
studying for careers in something besides law, do not attain real
literacy. Courses in media law do not prohibit structural thinking or broad normative discussions but such matters generally
occupy the background rather than the foreground.

Another influential way of dealing with freedom of the press
has been to historicize it. Historical studies of freedom of the
press (notably, Levy 1960; Siebert 1952), like legal studies, can
be superbly enlightening but tend to have an unanticipated effect. The best historical works seem to explain away freedom
of the press as an accident—no one ever chose it for the right
reasons, but people found it expedient to embrace it as a cause
from time to time; eventually, freedom of the press acquired the
force of tradition, though most citizens in the United States still
seem unable to articulate any justification for their belief in it
(Wyatt 1991). In a similar way, media critics (from Noam Chom-
sky on the left to Reed Irvine on the right) tend to explain away
freedom of the press as a rhetorical mystification.

The great contribution of *Four Theories* to the curriculum was
to carve out a terrain that encompasses both law and history
and to do it in a way that allows teachers and students to take
freedom of the press seriously. It does this in honest ways, by
insisting on attention to long-term change and deep structures
in both mentality and sociology (like the best legal scholarship
has done). It also does this in less defensible ways, most notably by being a bit slippery in its sense of "theory." Such vagueness may be necessary because the domains of the descriptive
and the normative cannot easily be housed in one tent. This is
an issue that will reappear regularly in the present book.

The curricular contribution of *Four Theories* is of obvious
importance to media scholars but perhaps to no one else. The
intellectual contribution of *Four Theories* is probably less obvi-

ous but it is of concern to a wider range of thinkers. By the mid-twentieth century, liberalism had reached a philosophical impasse. And, while political theory has moved beyond the impasse of liberalism, mainstream normative press theory in the United States really has not. To grasp this point, we should recapitulate briefly the moment in intellectual history at which *Four Theories* was written.

origin of IT

First, *Four Theories* postdated the demise of "natural rights" philosophy. The belief that the "rights of man [*sic*]" could be ascertained by reading the book of nature and that just, stable societies could be run on this basis became obsolescent sometime in the nineteenth century, a victim of positivism and naturalism and history and a lot of other thuggish elements. Natural rights were replaced by other kinds of rights—rights justified by utility and not necessarily by God or nature. Thus, the insides of political doctrines changed drastically while the outsides remained much the same—constitutional philosophy changed while most constitutions did not. People still talked about rights.

People understood these rights, like the older natural rights, as things that individuals had. And people continued to understand individuals to be like atoms—indivisible and basic, the stuff of which all other human paraphernalia (societies, cultures, classes) are made. These composite things all derived their properties from the atoms that composed them. This atomic theory of society was a bit off from the start, based as it was on bad physics in the service of bad sociology. But it worked for quite some time as an explanation of modernizing societies, until the point where the purpose of politics ceased to be the destruction of feudalism and became instead the fairer distribution of social goods through bureaucratic means. In the earlier politics, the actors were Thomas Paine, Voltaire, Thomas Jefferson, and "the common man." In the later politics, the actors were labor, the state, the school system, and of course the press. Put another way, the atomic notion of society ceased to make sense when politics became the stuff of institutions rather than of individuals.

Freedom of the press made reasonably good sense as a natural right. While the average person is not born with a printing press (unlike, say, a conscience or a tongue), still it was always pretty easy to justify freedom of the press as an extension of these other forms of freedom of expression. Moreover, in a world of atomic individuals, freedom of the press made tolerably good sense as a utilitarian right. God did not necessarily ordain this situation but people agreed that individuals free to print their ideas would be better suited to self-government. In both these renditions of liberal political philosophy, freedom of the press is a right of the individual, like freedom of speech or conscience; "the press" is nothing more than the printing press, the actual physical tool of printed expression. That is not what "the press" means anymore.

Now the press is understood to be an institution—a collection of news organizations that bears the same relationship to "the people" as does, say, the New York Stock Exchange. No one can pretend that the New York Stock Exchange *is* the people. Nor is the press equated with the people. Why then should we talk about freedom of the press? In liberal politics, corporate entities have freedom only as fictitious persons (i.e., individuals), or as depositories of the individual freedoms of actual persons. It is hard to think of the press as a fictitious person. And, if the press is a depository of the individual freedoms of its readers, then it certainly must have responsibilities. It is no more free to work against the interests of its readers than a publicly held corporation is free to work against the interests of its stockholders.

In intellectual terms, then, the classical liberal notion of freedom of the press had ceased to make sense by the time *Four Theories* was conceived. Ironically, this senseless notion had never been more urgently embraced. The immediate cause of the new passion for freedom of the press was World War II and its aftermath.

To Western thinkers, World War II seemed to say that the impasse in liberalism had a natural tendency to produce fascism. Modern Western countries such as Germany and Italy could adopt the symbols of the ancient empires and support autocrats of marginal sanity only because of a void in liberal politics generally; where people no longer agreed on the point of freedom, they would instinctively turn to strong leaders. This tendency had to be fought. But how? One recourse was to Marxisms of various sorts; but in the postwar West Joseph Stalin's Soviet Union seemed scarcely distinguishable from Adolf Hitler's Germany. Another remedy was a "neoliberal"[1] compromise in which the state abandoned the libertarian principle of minimal government and undertook to guarantee a certain level of social welfare—this is how most people understood Franklin D. Roosevelt's New Deal, and this is the direction most Western nations took.

Neoliberalism puts the press in a tough spot. On the one hand, the press is crucial as a bulwark of liberty and a check on corruption; as such, a great deal of journalistic autonomy is called for. On the other hand, the press, like all other institutions, public and private, has to be made to work for the public; freedom understood as the right to do what one will with one's property is a luxury that neoliberal societies can no longer afford their presses.

In other words, postwar thinkers at once embraced freedom of the press as a safeguard against fascism and denounced it as a prerogative of a propertied class or corporate interest over and against the people. Since the press was not the people, it became more intelligent to talk about the public's rights—the right to know, the right to free expression—rather than the press's rights. The press had responsibilities; the public had rights.

Hence the success of *Four Theories*. It portrays the impasse of liberalism in the postwar world; it captures the urgency of the moment, the sense of optimism associated with the defeat of fascism, as well as the dread of resurgent autocracy. It tells the story of liberalism's triumph over authoritarianism at the same time as it confesses that we no longer have a clear idea of what liberalism means for the press. It gives us historical and theoretical reasons to doubt the liberal worldview but does not offer an alternative. In this way, it stands at the end of a road. People have parked their cars here and wandered off into the brush but no one has returned with a map.

In this chapter, we will take a closer look at the composition of *Four Theories* from two perspectives: historical/biographical and theoretical. Historically, *Four Theories* is the product of a particular conjuncture of events and forces within Western history, the history of the news media, and the history of journalism education. Theoretically, *Four Theories* presents a schema of normative press theories that comes out of its specific historical moment but that can be argued against from a viewpoint either within or outside of its paradigm. We will present both critiques.

The Historical Moment of *Four Theories*

Scholarship is a product of its particular time; to understand why something was written we have to look at its historical context. But scholarship helps to create and perpetuate its time, as has *Four Theories of the Press* for almost forty years. The historical climate does not automatically imprint itself on scholars, but it does call up for expression certain views that often do no more than explain, justify, and accommodate that climate—in other words, the social, economic, and political reality. Scholarly production, far from being dispassionate writing by a class-free intelligentsia (to use Karl Mannheim's [1936] term), is anchored in that reality. *Four Theories,* by both its tone and format, represents itself as value-free scholarship, and many readers have accepted it as such. But a strong argument can be made that despite its value-free appearance it is driven by an agenda rooted in the context of its composition, specifically the cold war–

era global expansion of the U.S. model of privately owned for-profit media.

On one level of analysis, *Four Theories* was a product of liberal reactions against certain trends in the media. Indeed, the immediate stimulus for assembling the four essays came from the National Council of Churches (NCC), which had been sponsoring studies, funded by the Rockefeller Foundation, of ethics and responsibility in modern life. The NCC had become an important organization for thinkers from mainstream Protestant denominations who were critical of both secularism and unchecked corporate capitalism, especially ministers like Reinhold Niebuhr, who had been a member of the Hutchins Commission on Freedom of the Press (about which more below). As such, the NCC drew fire from both Protestant evangelicals and leading conservative business groups, including the National Association of Manufacturers (NAM).

The NCC had commissioned Wilbur Schramm to study responsibility in mass communications. As part of the project, Schramm enlisted the help of Fredrick S. Siebert and Theodore Peterson. Based on their earlier work, the three wrote "memoranda" that were spun off into *Four Theories*. Viewed this way, the book was an accidental add-on to a more "serious" work. Such a quick and casual collaboration is an unlikely candidate for scholarly longevity.

But *Four Theories* is not just a collaboration among three authors. It is scholarship that represents a certain way of understanding the relationship of the communications system to the society in which it operates. To be sure, the book's particular form and tone flow from the research interests of its authors as they work to explain this relationship, but that form and tone are also products of how material reality has cultivated their perspective. One key aspect of the reality that shaped *Four Theories* was the alliance between journalism educators and the communications business. On another level, the book responded to the cold war mentality of the late 1940s and 1950s and fed the perpetuation of that mentality. Both of these factors should be understood in the context of the long-term evolution of U.S. institutions.

In the twentieth century, industrial capitalism has been the uncontested, dominant institution in the United States. As such, it has fostered an ideological climate that works to sustain the general interests of capital and the "free market" as an economic system. This has been evident, for example, in the political sphere. As *Four Theories* itself pointed out (although using different language), the rise of private enterprise as an economic form during the seventeenth and eighteenth centuries provoked changes in the political realm that launched state systems reflecting the aspirations and demands of a new, ascending class. The dominant institution reshaped other institutions, among them the judicial, communications, and educational systems. Education is an especially relevant case.

Whereas education in the medieval period was almost exclusively in the hands of the clergy, the new capitalist economic order successfully secularized most instruction. In the United States, for example, a tax-based public school system complemented by private schools and colleges developed. The purpose and content of education shifted, as had the form and objective of the state. Control of higher education on the broadest level, as well as on the specifics of curricula and faculty hiring, responded to the general demands of the dominant institution. Not surprisingly, the educational system did not challenge the basic premises of the industrial capitalist economic order. The adequacy and legitimacy of the order were taken for granted. Any debate that took place was over how to make the economy operate more efficiently. Radicalism had no place.

The rise of journalism education should be understood in this context. The academy provided intellectual support for the economic order, but it was not clear how far the academy should go to provide professional job training. Medicine and law were firm parts of university curricula but in the early decades of this

century a bitter contest arose over providing vocational training for newspaper reporters and copy editors. The result of that
debate was the establishment, almost exclusively in tax-support-
ed universities, of many journalism curricula that trained students for entry-level positions on the editorial and occasionally
the advertising and management sides of the newspaper business. The aim of journalism schools was not only to teach tech-
niques, though most courses did precisely that, but also implicitly to cultivate students who would accept the basic premises
of the business and their roles in it.

Journalism schools tended to be cordial with the working
press. Professional experience was almost universally a requirement for faculty status since papers felt good training could be
provided only by those who had direct hands-on knowledge of
the trade. Faculty who also did research often worked on in-
dustry-related problems. Friendly relations with the press helped
to insure financial support for journalism curricula and jobs for
graduates. Some publishers, for various reasons, remained suspicious of the value of college-level journalism training. Nonetheless, journalism programs broadly supported the business.
They did their best to prepare the kinds of people publishers
wanted to hire, just as universities in general broadly supported, and indeed helped to form, ideology in resonance with the
dominant institution.

The authors of *Four Theories* worked in this climate. The
University of Illinois, as Siebert says in unpublished autobio-
graphical notes, was a "conservative land grant institution." Its
journalism program and faculty, though much finer than most
at the time, had aims that differed little from those elsewhere.

Siebert's career exemplifies the close link between education
and the industry. After some newspaper experience in the early
1920s, Siebert attended law school at Illinois and was admitted
to the bar in 1929. That same year he was hired by the journalism program and became the legal counsel for the Illinois Press
Association. Later he took on similar duties for the National

Editorial Association and the Inland Daily Press Association. At the request of Colonel Robert McCormick, and on behalf of the *Chicago Tribune,* Siebert wrote a friend of the U.S. Supreme Court brief in the landmark case of *Near v. Minnesota* (1931), in which the Court overturned as "prior restraint" a Minnesota law allowing the suppression of malicious and scandalous publications. Slightly more than a decade later, as director of Illinois's School of Journalism, Siebert assisted the *Tribune*'s law firm when it intervened in the Justice Department's antitrust suit against the Associated Press (AP), a case precipitated when Colonel McCormick used his veto power to prevent a rival paper from joining the news service. Later, McCormick was partially to subsidize, as did the American Newspaper Publishers Association (ANPA), Siebert's research in England on the British origins of the First Amendment, which led to Siebert's *Freedom of the Press in England, 1476–1776* (1952). Siebert's contribution to journalism training was recognized in 1944 when he was elected president of the American Association of Schools and Departments of Journalism. He later helped found the American Council on Education for Journalism to evaluate and accredit journalism programs. Siebert was responsible for bringing Theodore Peterson from the Kansas State University journalism program to the Illinois journalism faculty in 1948, and he became Peterson's teacher and dissertation advisor.

Intimations of what would become the *Four Theories* schema can be found in Siebert's earlier work. Siebert worked on *Freedom of the Press in England* for almost twenty years. His study of three centuries of English history disclosed, he said in the introduction, "three theories of the function of the press in society, particularly in relation to organized government" (1952, 5). He called them the Tudor-Stuart, the Blackstone-Mansfield, and the Camden-Erskine-Jefferson theories. This special use of the term "theory" was easily adapted to a modern setting for he said that "three additional positions on the relation of the government to the press" had also appeared. The first was the position on the "allowable area of freedom taken by the Supreme Court . . . in a series of decisions since 1919." The second was "the theory of the Hutchins Commission, [a] theory of social responsibility of the press." The third was that "of the Communist government of Soviet Russia" (1952, 11–12).

Siebert modified this six-theory schema as early as 1953. In a speech to accept the research award of Kappa Tau Alpha, the national honorary journalism society, he described four theories "of the function and purpose of the mass media [that] form the basis for the communication patterns of modern society": authoritarian, libertarian, social responsibility, and Soviet communist (1953, 659). This became the blueprint for the volume published in 1956 by the University of Illinois Press.

The third coauthor, Wilbur Schramm, had been director of the journalism school at the University of Iowa from 1943 to 1947 and a vice president of the American Association of Schools and Departments of Journalism, where he had worked with Siebert. Schramm came to the University of Illinois in 1947 to develop a doctoral program with Siebert and to direct the newly created Institute of Communications Research. Schramm's plan called for the Institute to conduct internally and externally funded research.

Schramm's career points up another facet of the context of *Four Theories:* the cold war and the U.S. global agenda. During World War II, Schramm had worked for the Office of War Information, the Navy Department, the War Department, and the U.S. Armed Forces Institute. In the postwar period, his public vita shows he also was a consultant on psychological warfare to the U.S. Air Force and a consultant to the State Department, the Army Operations Research Office, the Defense Department, and the U.S. Information Agency. In the mid-1950s, he chaired the Defense Secretary's advisory board on specialized warfare.

Schramm's output in this period clearly reflected these involvements. He co-authored *The Reds Take a City* (1951) about the occupation of Seoul by North Korean forces. The Air Force funded research for the volume. The following year, under an Army contract, he produced *FEC* [Far East Command] *Psychological Warfare Operations: Radio,* a report declassified in 1966. Schramm's reader, *The Process and Effects of Mass Communication,* first published in 1954, "originated [the foreword said] in the United States Information Agency's need for a book of background materials which could be used in training some of the agency's new employees." This widely used college text, like Schramm's other pioneering anthologies, *Communications in Modern Society* (1948) and *Mass Communications* (1949), is mute about the economic function of media as an integral part of the free enterprise system in the United States, including their role in reproducing capital, an absence quite in keeping with his anticommunist activities.

Parts of *Four Theories* can be found in Schramm's work from this period. In 1955, under a contract between Illinois's Institute of Communications Research and the U.S. Information Agency (USIA), Schramm assembled four working papers on propaganda theory. Schramm's contribution, "The Soviet Concept of 'Psychological' Warfare," has sections on Soviet media that are remarkably similar to passages in *Four Theories.*

While Schramm criticized the Soviet system, others at the time found much to worry about in the United States. Studies in the 1930s and 1940s had demonstrated that the media, under certain circumstances, had power to change attitudes and behavior. How did this power mesh with the traditional understanding of laissez-faire media operation? Advertising, persuasion, and wartime propaganda, for example, confirmed that media, and the entities that owned and used them, were not merely benign purveyors of truth but in fact had their own agendas. Many observers worried that news and fact were being superseded by entertainment and image and that profit-driven media debased the level of the general culture. Would these concerns require rethinking how media should be operated?

Apart from the matter of individual and social effects, companies owning communications media had run afoul of antitrust laws. In 1945, the Supreme Court found that the Associated Press by-laws illegally restrained trade and that AP members had conspired to thwart competition. Newspaper publishers had earlier tried to discourage news broadcasts on radio. In 1938, the Justice Department accused eight film companies of conspiring to restrain competition in the distribution and exhibition of pictures. The case was settled a decade later with a victory for the plaintiff. The threat of antitrust action caused the National Broadcasting Company in the early 1940s to dispose of one of its radio networks. AT&T was attacked for practices that sought to discourage competition in the manufacture and sale of telephone equipment and provision of long distance service. In addition, trends in media revealed increasing concentration of ownership and, in the press, the substantial growth of one-newspaper cities. The media, regardless of whether they carried advertising, were firmly embedded in the business system.

Yet media businesses reacted angrily to even sympathetic criticism. In its 1947 report, *A Free and Responsible Press,* the Hutchins Commission on Freedom of the Press (discussed in chapter 3) raised controversial questions about the role of the media in society but stressed the need to maintain a privately owned, profit-driven communications system. The report cautioned that a laissez-faire attitude would no longer suffice because mass communication had assumed a previously unknown social, economic, and political importance. Although some quarters of the press vilified these findings, the Commission made clear that it had not invented these views but had relied on what media owners and executives had said. Still, the notion that media should behave responsibly, that they had moral obligations, was abhorrent to those who clung to free-market principles. The controversy was but a replay of a larger debate about whether business in general had any responsibilities at all to society, beyond a primary obligation to owners and investors. For advocates of responsibility, the benevolent business theme was seen as correcting the robber baron image and the bad marks the capitalist system had chalked up in the Great Depression.

Globally, World War II had thrust the United States into the role of world leader. As such, it spearheaded the establishment of international instruments that were to recast the world according to its own plans. The United Nations, United Nations Educational, Scientific, and Cultural Organization (UNESCO), the General Agreement on Tariffs and Trade (GATT), the Organization for Economic Cooperation and Development (OECD), and the Universal Copyright Convention, among others, became sites in which U.S. policy worked itself out. U.S. definitions of free flow and freedom of information were written into international charters "under tutelage of American experts," according to Siebert (*Four Theories,* 68, hereinafter cited as FT). Meanwhile, the U.S. government, assisted by media interests, worked hard overseas to eliminate tariff and nontariff barriers to the export of American media products, in part because of their propaganda value in the cold war. But this campaign also was part of a larger program to make the world safe for American business. National development overseas was defined as growth along a capitalist path paralleling expansion of mass media facilities that were to be privately owned, profit-driven, advertising-based, and independent of the state (but not of capital). Ideally, they were to be little mirrors of the U.S. system.

A critical stance toward the role of the media in the global expansion of capitalism and U.S. ideology in the postwar era leads us to an equally critical assessment of *Four Theories of the Press.* This book provided an intellectual veneer for what often had been nuts-and-bolts journalism training. It masterfully explained, from its own perspective, why media systems are what they are, and it catalogued historical relations between media and the state. *Four Theories* was not just a product of the way its three authors viewed these matters. More accurately, they were articulate spokesmen for a point of view conditioned by relations between journalism education and the press business, between the academy and the economic system, and between two superpowers locked in a cold war. The book staked out a field of inquiry, defined the terms of discourse, and structured the way the academy and those who pass through it understand the communication system.

Theoretical Shortcomings

Whatever its genesis, *Four Theories* is designed to present an apparently timeless structure of ideas. And it is as a schema of "theories" that it has been most influential. The remainder of this chapter will focus on the inadequacies of this schema. Before we undertake that task, though, it is important to mention that *Four Theories* is simultaneously engaged in another project, one that often runs at cross-purposes with its schema. Specifically, this is the task of *Weltanschauung* analysis.

The notion of *Weltanschauung*, or "worldview," is central to the thinking of Jay Jensen, a fourth member of the Illinois faculty (and subsequently head of the journalism department) whose influence can be seen here and there in *Four Theories*. *Four Theories* was published just as Jensen was completing his dissertation, "Liberalism, Democracy, and the Mass Media," a work that has never been formally published but which might be seen as the more refined and scholarly version of *Four Theories*.

Jensen's chief argument is that the worldview, to use the less cumbersome term, is the proper explanatory motif for the legal, cultural, political, and institutional history of the media. The worldview is the collective vision that a civilization brings to everything it does. In more contemporary scholarly parlance, then, a worldview is like a discourse, mentalité, or ideology. It is like a discourse in that it constructs in advance the terms of any discussion that will take place; it is like a mentalité in that it is comprehensive; and it is like an ideology in that it has political and moral import. The contours of a worldview are discoverable through a close reading of the most articulate thinkers of a civilization, especially its philosophers.

Western civilization's worldview in the modern era has been liberalism, initially classical liberalism and then neoliberalism. Thus, the history of the Western media and the laws and policies that govern them should be understood in terms of the unfolding of the liberal worldview. This story can be told through the great books and great thinkers—John Locke, Jean-Jacques Rousseau, Thomas Jefferson, and John Stuart Mill, of course, but also Isaac Newton, Charles Darwin, Sigmund Freud, and Albert Einstein.

Jensen's work, while similar to the *Four Theories* project, is also distinct. Like *Four Theories,* he works on the most general level and his analysis emphasizes ideas over material causes. But a worldview is not a "theory." Worldviews are historically specific and not abstractable or generalizable. So the worldview of the modern West is just that: it is not a theory that can be applied to, say, ancient Athens.

One of the tensions that makes *Four Theories* interesting (and bedeviling) is the unacknowledged discord between history and theory. Jensen's project chooses history and, though it can be criticized for many things, it retains a conceptual lucidity that is not present in *Four Theories,* which tries to work on both history and theory at the same time, a much trickier proposition.

Still, the most familiar aspect of *Four Theories* is its schema of theories. On this level the book can be effectively critiqued in at least two ways. It can be critiqued according to the internal inadequacies of its categories and terms of analysis; it can also be critiqued as an expression of a particular ideology.

Internal Inconsistencies and Inadequacies

The conceptual framework of *Four Theories* is designed to facilitate the introduction of a vocabulary for discussing media-in-society. It achieves this with elegance but in the process introduces some imprecisions and oversimplifications. To begin, we may deal quickly with the term "theory." It is clearly not used in this book in the scientific sense, which implies rigorous examination and testing of hypotheses under controlled conditions. On the contrary, and given Siebert's background, the term is drawn from law. It is synonymous with "explanation" and "rationale."

Moreover, *Four Theories* does not offer four theories: it offers one theory with four examples. Its theory, to paraphrase, is that in its structure, policy, and behavior the communications system reflects the society in which it operates and that society can be categorically defined by a coherent philosophy (FT 1–2). That is the basic postulate of the book. The authors provide evidence to support that theory, not to test it.

Within this overarching theory, the authors construct a schema of the different available philosophies that can define a society and its communications system. They offer four exemplars of this other kind of theory, namely, the authoritarian theory, the libertarian theory, the social responsibility theory, and the Soviet communist theory. The overarching theory (in the scientific sense) has problems that will be explored below. The schema of the four specific theories (or philosophies) has other problems.

First, the four theories do not have the same level of historical concreteness. Authoritarianism is a vague term applied to a very broad range of distinguishable press theories; libertarianism refers to a more concrete sensibility in the modern West; social responsibility theory refers to an attempt by specific thinkers in a specific historical conjuncture to formulate a professional ideology; and the Soviet communist theory likewise has a high level of historical specificity, though it is taken to epitomize a broader range of thinking, namely Marxism. Thus, the four theories are really quite different things, historically speaking. They have operated at different levels and in some cases have coexisted with each other—the social responsibility theory characterizes a professional attitude that has resided within libertarian attitudes toward the press, for instance (though with some tension).

Second (and this follows from the above), the four theories are not all theories in the same sense. Authoritarianism, for instance, is really not a theory at all but a set of practices—a point we shall take up again in chapter 2. In his chapter on authoritarianism, Siebert mentions a great many authoritarian societies and institutions, all somewhat different, then imputes a common set of attitudes to them, thereby constructing the "authoritarian theory." In some cases he is justified, in others he acknowledges shortcomings. But it is not really the "authoritarian theory" that defines authoritarianism; rather, the defining factor is the practical fact of a concentration in the exercise of power.

Siebert uses a different approach in constructing the libertarian theory. He derives the theory from a discussion of specific thinkers—Milton, Jefferson, and Mill—who have canonical status; libertarianism thus has real existence as a theory, though it has often been combined with authoritarian practices. (The lack of fit between theory and practice is a recurring problem in *Four Theories*.)

The last two theories are far more grounded in twentieth-century historical realities. They are also more explicitly formulated as theories of press operation. The social responsibility theory was constructed to serve as a set of operating principles for a profession; the Soviet communist theory was likewise constructed to serve a state (or party) apparatus. Thus, because these theories are so specific, they are also less universal and hence less exclusive. Social responsibility theory, for instance, has occupied a niche within libertarianism, despite some disagreement on basic premises: in the United States, journalists tend to proclaim responsibility while publishers tend to protect property rights. It is not impossible, likewise, to imagine journalists operating under a notion of social responsibility in a state operating under a form of Soviet communism.

Third, then, the presentation of four distinct and equivalent theories of the press gives the incorrect impression that any press system will be defined by one coherent theory of the press. While this is a useful assumption for abstract discussions of press operation, it is not especially helpful for discussing specific historical situations in which theories always overlap and in which the various actors are often motivated by quite different notions.

Fourth, each of the theories—but especially the first two—is oversimplified. The book uses a four-part scheme for identifying the theories: each theory has a notion of the human, the state, knowledge, and truth. Authoritarianism, then, has a notion of an incomplete human individual, a state that is an end in itself, knowledge that is difficult and available to only a few, and an absolute truth. Libertarianism has the opposite—a complete individual, a state that is a means to an end, knowledge for the people, and relative truth. But in each particular case there are examples that directly contradict the theory. Thomas Hobbes, surely an authoritarian, had the same notions of the individual, knowledge, and truth as John Locke, surely a liberal. The Hobbesian state is authoritarian, but as a policing force among warring individuals, not as an expression of the spirit of a people, as in Georg W. F. Hegel. Likewise, fascism, surely authoritarian, had a notion of truth that seems patently opportunistic. On the basis of an absolutist notion of truth, Plato, also an authoritarian, glamorized Socrates, whom Plato depicted as an anarchist. Some liberals invoked a corporatist notion of society or community, quite distinct from the Lockean individualism that characterizes the libertarian theory. The examples could be multiplied. The point is that each of the four theories is oversimplified.

This challenges the link between theory and policy. It is possible—Hobbes is a good case—to share all the fundamental postulates of libertarian theory as presented by Siebert and still call for authoritarian policies. We might well ask, "Where is a theory of the press?" or "Who has a theory of the press?" *Four Theories* does not really examine these questions, and we are left to ponder whether any particular theory really defines any particular situation. Did "libertarianism" define the press system of the nineteenth-century United States? If so, was it because people (the public, the press, the state) believed in the libertarian theory? Or was it because the system (ownership structures, market considerations, legal requirements) was de facto libertarian? This is a compelling case in point, because few doubt that the nineteenth-century press was more "libertarian" than its twentieth-century counterpart; but fewer doubt that legal protections for free expression and public tolerance of dissident views are stronger in the twentieth than in the nineteenth century, when mainstream partisans defended slavery on racial grounds, called openly for attacks on Mormons, abolitionists, and the foreign-born, and assumed without question that women should not vote. If "libertarianism" came naturally from the system but was not reflected in beliefs, then why call it a theory?

Fifth, *Four Theories* pays too little attention to concentrations of power in the private sector. In most of its chapters, the authors (without acknowledging the fact) employ classical liberal notions of individuals and the state, in which the "private" is the realm of freedom and is identified with the individual and the "public" is the realm of control and is identified with the state. As a result, "society" is used almost interchangeably with "state" as a term to designate collective human existence, giving the impression that there are no collective entities outside of the state. But in most political theory the state is only one element of control, while other elements operate in what is called the private realm or civil society—in schools, churches, families, and workplaces.

This points up, finally, the fundamental conceptual problem with *Four Theories:* it defines the four theories from within one of the four theories—classical liberalism. It is, in fact, classical liberalism (or libertarianism) that generates the vocabulary used to discuss all the other theories because it is specifically within classical liberalism that the political world is divided into individuals versus society or the state. By contrast, premodern notions of community or polity deny the salience of the individual versus society opposition. Likewise, Marxism and postmodernist notions

of the state and subjectivity are at odds with liberal notions of individuality. Such notions cannot be accommodated by a schema that defines theories within a liberal vocabulary.

This theoretical grounding is never made explicit within the book. This presents a problem in that, while it is certainly defensible to dissect normative theories from within a particular framework, a reader is ill-served if this is not made apparent. Moreover, a critical reader might impute dishonest motives to the whole enterprise, particularly if that reader is grounded in one of the slighted paradigms.

Silences and Absences

If we question the primacy of the political in the communications system, then we are likely to find *Four Theories* misleading. The assumption of *Four Theories,* like the assumption of classical liberalism, is that freedom of the press (or, more generally, the normative role of the press) is a political thing. Put another way, *Four Theories* and classical liberalism assume that we have freedom of the press if we are free to discuss political matters in print without state suppression. Freedom of the press is defined as political because the press is understood as political. Many believe, however, that the communications system in capitalist societies is not simply political but also and perhaps primarily economic and that what liberals call freedom is not meaningful without another kind of freedom. A truly free press would be free not just of state intervention but also of market forces and ownership ties and a host of other material bonds. This point of view is stated in *Four Theories* (most familiarly under the notion of "positive freedom" in Peterson's chapter on social responsibility theory), but the critique of liberal press systems it inspires is largely absent.

The implicit adoption of a liberal framework (described above) entails deficiencies in the book's usefulness as a description of how communications systems are owned, organized, and operated. These deficiencies are exemplified in its focus on newspapers to the almost complete exclusion of other media (although it is mysterious how, under the libertarian and social responsibility theories, the recorded music and filmed entertainment businesses, to cite just two media, participate in "the search for truth"). The shortcomings are located more concretely in the way the book situates all media in relation to the economic institution and the state. In arguing that "in the last analysis the difference between press systems is one of philosophy" (FT 2), the book disregards the material existence of media. Similarly, in contending that "the press always takes on the form and coloration of the social and political structures within which it operates" (FT 1), the book slights fundamental economic aspects and rules out seeing the communications system as an economic instrument with an economic role to play. Ignoring its own presumptions and presenting itself as a work of objective scholarship, *Four Theories* actually mystifies the role of media in society, particularly capitalist society.

A fundamental flaw in the book is the use of a terminology that both promotes a white/black, good/bad understanding and colors how evidence is assembled and interpreted. The book argues that what it all comes down to is that there are really only two "theories," only two environments in which media can operate—libertarian and authoritarian, which to the authors mean free from state control and controlled by the state. The other two theories, the authors say, are but modifications of these two opposing and irreconcilable poles (FT 2). The libertarian theory becomes, with conscience and moral trappings, the social responsibility theory. The authoritarian theory becomes, in its most severe and repressive manifestation, the Soviet communist theory. We should remember that *Four Theories* implicitly defines freedom and control only on the political plane, as characterizations of relationships to state power, and is mostly silent on other kinds of power.

The line of argument in the book is similar to that made by

opponents of government regulation throughout the economy. They claim that deregulation is necessary so that businesses can be free to respond to the demands of an unfettered market, implying that this "natural" state of affairs will amount to an uncontrolled use of resources. But there can be no uncontrolled use of resources because the allocation of productive resources always presumes some kind of control over those resources. What deregulation advocates actually want is a shift in where that regulation occurs—that is, where decisions are made, by whom, and on what standards. In practice, they want the regulation of resources to be entirely in the private sector, by business people, using a profit-motivated standard. They want complete authority over the factors of production. Decisions about competition, price, safety, quantity, and quality, they say, should result from how businesses read the market, rather than from government edicts that seek to protect the public or assure more equitable distribution.

The libertarian theory, as *Four Theories* constructs it, assumes that in the absence of state control, the media are free, that deregulation (or nonregulation) necessarily coincides with liberty, and that the state is the only possible source of obstruction to media operation. What is troubling about this reasoning is that it does not concede even a theoretical benefit from rules a democratic government may enact and, much more importantly, it does not acknowledge that there are sources of control other than the state, notably the "free market" itself.

It is this basic dichotomy, state versus media (or state versus private interest), that frames *Four Theories*. The dichotomy is the locus of tension that, the authors claim, explains how media operate and whether they are "free" to serve the public or whether they are instruments that social forces use to manipulate the public. Far from being an analysis of this problem, the book actually is part of the problem it addresses. This is so because the book falls into the conceptual trap of defining freedom with the very terms that one of its theories uses to define freedom. Under libertarian theory, freedom exists when there is no coercion by the state. Freedom of the press exists when the state stays out of media ownership, operation, and regulation. Since the book adopts the worldview of one of the theories it presumes to examine, the book biases its own case and necessarily concludes that any system that does not measure up to this worldview lacks freedom.

In *Four Theories,* all conflict is understood on the classical liberal continuum of individual versus the state. Thus, of the libertarian theory Siebert says that "the underlying purpose of the media [is] to help discover truth, to assist in the process of solving political and social problems by presenting all manner of evidence and opinion as the basis for decisions. *The essential characteristic of this process was its freedom from government controls or domination*" (FT 51, emphasis added). Peterson reports that the "functions of the press under social responsibility theory are basically the same as those under libertarian theory," but that occasionally the press "has been deficient in performing those tasks" (FT 74). The "theory holds that the *government must not merely allow freedom;* it must also actively promote it" (FT 95, emphasis added). Schramm writes that "the American feels blessed with his free press" (FT 105). It is true that Siebert's discussion of libertarian theory is a normative view of what the press should be doing, whereas Peterson's chapter on social responsibility theory (and Schramm's on the Soviet communist) is more descriptive. This, however, does not minimize the defect of the book's theoretical posture, which defines liberty as the absence of state restraint.

What is the purpose of this liberty? It provides the environment in which the press can exercise its "right and duty . . . to serve as an extralegal check on government." When Siebert writes that "the press [has] to be completely free from control or domination by those elements which it [is] to guard against" (FT 56), he means government, not any elements in the "private sector."

Underlying the authors' presumptions about the state versus individual continuum is a belief that private ownership of the media is the only acceptable form and that independence from outside control is predicated on a sound financial base. Siebert concedes, though, that "the problem of the economic support of the mass media was never squarely faced by libertarian theorists" (FT 52), but he does not tell readers why this was so. He merely says that "they trusted the capitalist system of private enterprise to find a way" (FT 52).

There is a dilemma here, and it comes from the (characteristically liberal) failure to recognize forms of power other than that of the state. How can the press, to use Siebert's words again, be "completely free from control or domination" when it is part of the business system and driven by the same kinds of economic concerns and motives that drive other businesses? The press cannot logically be free from capital because it *is* capital in form and use. A press regulated by the state, we are told, cannot be free and "ever vigilant to spot and expose any arbitrary or authoritarian practice" (FT 56). The corollary to that must be, although unstated by the authors, that the press driven by capital cannot be expected to provide a thorough critique of the economic system or to offer alternatives because it is not "free from control or domination" by capital. Naturally, from its very beginning, the capital-driven press did not have as its aim to be a watchdog over the system of which it is a part. Watchdogs do not bite their owners.

Part of this conceptual trap is that the book has no room for media controlled by neither state nor private capital. Falling into limbo, for example, are newspapers and periodicals owned and run by labor unions, political movements and parties, not-for-profit organizations, and religious bodies. Since these do not necessarily "service the economic system" and are not profit-driven, are we to infer that they do not meet the criteria of freedom established in *Four Theories?* If privately owned, profit-seeking media are free, then are we to infer that broadcasting stations are less free if they are owned by community groups, nonprofit corporations, universities, religious groups, and municipalities? The book is largely silent on such media but the occasional mention supports that inference. For instance, Siebert tells us with chauvinistic firmness that "the American system of broadcasting [on the capitalist model] is more consistent with libertarian principles than the others" (FT 65), meaning those in France, Great Britain, and Canada that were operating on a public service basis when the book was written.

We are forced to conclude from descriptions of media systems in *Four Theories* that only private capital imposes no restraint and that it is a benign organizational form. Businesses that own and operate media respond rationally to market demands and provide the goods and services the public wants. Thus, again Siebert notes: "Anyone with sufficient capital could start a communication enterprise . . . [and] the success of the enterprise would be determined by the public which it sought to serve" (FT 52). To this very thinking we can direct the same criticism Schramm levels at what he calls Marxism's "amazing confidence in explaining great areas of human behavior on the basis of a small set of economic facts" (FT 107).[2]

The theoretical and ideological bias of the volume also is apparent in the authors' terminology. The names of the theories themselves are determined by the assumption that the relationship to the state (and not ownership structures) is key. An authoritarian system is called that because the press operates to support the power of the state. The Soviet communist media system is called that because it follows the policy of the Soviet communist state. (Actually, Schramm is in error on this point because it was the party that was the locus of power, not the state.) The media system in the United States is called libertarian rather than capitalist, arguably a more appropriate label, because the authors do not assign names based on the media system's dominant ownership form or function but only on the system's relation to the state. The same inclination appears in routine word usage throughout the book. The terms "capital," "capitalist," "capitalism," and "capitalistic" appear twice as often in the chapter on the Soviet communist theory than they do in the three chapters dealing with the authoritarian, libertarian, and social responsibility theories—press systems based predominantly on private capital. Schramm uses these terms almost two dozen times in recounting Soviet criticisms of the press in countries with capitalist market systems. Siebert and Peterson prefer other terms, such as "private enterprise" and "private ownership," with Peterson particularly fond of "business," "businessman," and "business class." The term "profit-driven" appears neither in the chapter on the libertarian theory nor in the one on social responsibility theory. "Commodity," in the sense of audiences sold to advertisers and media products sold to consumers, does not appear in the volume at all. This underscores the book's silence on the material structure of libertarian and social-responsibility press systems.

The book criticizes media operating under libertarian and social responsibility theories but in a genial way. There seems to be nothing structurally wrong with those media systems but certain objectionable practices can be corrected or ameliorated with attention to ethics and moral standards. By contrast, under authoritarian and Soviet communist theories, the media have fundamental structural deficiencies because they are agents of state power. Schramm says that "mass communications, from the beginning of the proletarian revolution, were conceived of instrumentally. . . . The media were . . . instruments to be controlled by the state" (FT 116). Siebert points out that under "all authoritarian theories of governments . . . the mass media were assigned a specific role" (FT 16–17) by the state, that is, they were instrumentalized as well. Media under libertarian and social responsibility theories, according to the authors, serve primarily "to help discover truth" and "to raise conflict to the plane of discussion" (FT 7). As Schramm phrases it, "In our system, mass communication is a service rather than an instrument, and is used . . . not for preconceived ends" (FT 146). There is a blind-spot in the authors' argument: media under libertarian and so-cial responsibility theories also are instrumentalized—not by the state but rather by private capital. Media are instruments as-signed specific roles, namely to reproduce and multiply capital, to serve the interests of capital, because they are owned and di-rected by capital. This is true ipso facto. If it were not, then our media system would be owned and operated by philanthrop-ic agencies and not-for-profit corporations.

In *Four Theories* then, we have a case of prominent scholars who have uncritically accepted the very ideological mystifica-tion the media owners propound to explain their own existence. The myth of the free press in the service of society exists be-cause it is in the interest of media owners to perpetuate it. *Four Theories* seems to explore this myth; actually, it provides an in-tellectual ratification of it.

A Legacy Revisited

The following chapters will anatomize *Four Theories* from a va-riety of perspectives. Chapter 2 examines Siebert's chapters on authoritarianism and libertarianism. In addition to critiquing his account from both a historical and philosophical standpoint, we try to relate some recent developments in the historiogra-phy of liberalism and in the elaboration of liberal theory since the 1950s. Chapter 3 presents a series of arguments about social responsibility theory and attempts to assess its historical impact and continuing relevance in the United States. Chapter 4 ad-dresses Marxist and other alternative media systems.

The final chapter and the conclusion of the book deal with the problems of doing normative press theory at the end of the twentieth century. Much has changed since the publication of *Four Theories*. The cold war has ended, "the press" is a term that makes less sense than "the media," and a raft of new social prob-lems has been added to the political and intellectual agenda of academics. For decades scholars have pondered revising *Four Theories* by adding a fifth or sixth. We pose a more fundamental question: whether the whole enterprise needs to be rethought.

Notes

1. By neoliberalism here and throughout the book, we refer to a specific mutation from classical liberalism, not to a contemporary political label.

2. Schramm's discussion of the Soviet communications system searches for the kind of theoretical foundation that Siebert constructs for libertarianism from Milton, Locke, Mill, and others. The problem Schramm encounters is trying to link the Soviet system (organized by Stalin) back through V. I. Lenin to roots in Karl Marx. Schramm explains that Marx's thought underwent "mutations," that Marx "expressed dissatisfaction with what his followers were doing to his ideas," and that "the tradition of Marx has undergone profound changes" (FT 106). After introducing such disclaimers, Schramm nonetheless proceeds to link Marx to Soviet practice by revealing "at least three sets of ideas" from Marx that have been "the foundation stones for everything his Soviet followers have built." In the discussion, Schramm easily shifts terminology, using "Marx," "Marxism," and "Marxist" interchangeably and without qualification. Schramm's analysis of Marx's ideas, however, is not built on citations to Marx's work, except in one case. It is built on a cold war, Western analysis of that work and in some cases on a Stalinist interpretation of it. The fallacy in Schramm's discussion is that he accepts uncritically the Soviet claim that its system is rooted in Marx, rather than inquiring into the validity of that claim.

2

Authoritarianism and Liberalism

❖ ❖ ❖

Fredrick Siebert, the author of the first two chapters of *Four Theories,* "The Authoritarian Theory" and "The Libertarian Theory," is best known for his magnum opus on freedom of the press in England in the three centuries from the introduction of the printing press to the American Revolution (Siebert 1952). Still a standard work, that volume furnishes the framework for Siebert's contributions to *Four Theories.* The history of early modern England drives Siebert's analysis of authoritarianism and libertarianism in a fairly obvious way. Many of Siebert's examples of authoritarian practices come from Tudor-Stuart England, and most of his examples of libertarian thought are furnished by the great English liberal thinkers. As a narrative of English legal history, these chapters still speak with authority.

But Siebert's historical work is a bit different from the overall *Four Theories* project. English history is concrete and particular but *Four Theories* aims for the timeless and universal; Siebert satisfied these demands by abstracting libertarianism from a particular moment in its English career and globalizing it. At the same time, he constructed an authoritarian theory that was a flat negation of libertarianism—a mirror image, as it were. The result is a simplified version of liberalism and an authoritarian-

*liberalism simplified,
authoritarianism were mirror image*

ism that has little historical reality. Siebert's versions of these theories have a certain classroom elegance, of course, but can generate some confusion (especially in the case of authoritarianism) and are insufficiently nuanced. Liberalism is really more diverse and more alive and authoritarianism less reasoned and less dead than his characterizations would allow.

This chapter treats both the authoritarian and libertarian theories, but it will be clear to the astute reader that it is primarily about liberalism. Because Siebert's authoritarian theory is substantially a negative version of his libertarian theory, it would hardly support a chapter of its own. The chapter begins with a critique of "The Authoritarian Theory." We argue that Siebert's authoritarianism is a poorly constructed straw man and that authoritarianism is better thought of as a set of practices than as a theory. We also argue that, as a set of practices, authoritarianism can be found not just in autocratic states but in governments that proclaim a liberal or democratic set of core beliefs.

Next, the chapter tackles "The Libertarian Theory." Here we argue that Siebert conflated other philosophies of free expression, like antinomianism and republicanism, with libertarianism. We note the decline of liberal theory, as Siebert did, but remark on its revival in the years since the publication of *Four Theories* and comment on its persistence as a style of legal argument and reasoning. We discuss contemporary variations of liberalism, such as egalitarianism and communitarianism. Finally, we note contemporary challenges to liberalism in the form of multiculturalism and postmodernism.

The Dilemma of Authoritarianism

Four Theories defines authoritarianism as a theory, obviously. The book argues that authoritarians embrace (consciously or unconsciously) a set of premises about individuals, society, the state, and truth and knowledge. Thus, while authoritarians are quite diverse historically, it is implied that they are united by this common theory. This implication is certainly questionable, and we will return to it. First, though, we will review the authoritarian theory as *Four Theories* outlines it.

The premises of the authoritarian theory are given as follows:

> Man [*sic*] could attain his [*sic*] full potentialities only as a member of society. . . . [Thus] the group took on an importance greater than that of the individual. . . . The state . . . [is] the highest expression of group organization. . . . In and through the state, man achieves his ends; without the state, man remains a primitive being. . . . [The state] derived its power . . . through a process not generally capable of complete human analysis. . . . Knowledge was discoverable through mental effort. Men differed widely in their ability to utilize mental processes. . . . "Wise men" . . . should become leaders in organized society. . . . In addition, the authoritarian's theory demanded a unity of intellectual activity since only through unity could the state operate successfully for the good of all. (FT 10–11)

Summarized this baldly, the authoritarian theory seems unproblematical. The premises are certainly consistent with one another—there is nothing in the assertion that the state is "the highest expression of group organization" that contradicts the premise that knowledge is achieved "through mental effort." The practical implications of such a theory are also apparent: anyone who maintained all these premises must be an authoritarian and must see an urgent need for state regulation of thought and expression.

But *Four Theories* asks a bit more from authoritarianism. First, it asks that all authoritarian *thinkers* share all of these premises rather than just some. Second, it asks that all authoritarian *practitioners* also be adherents of authoritarianism the theory. Neither of these demands is reasonable.

To begin with, we can find in *Four Theories* a twinned opposite assertion for each authoritarian premise. On the nature of "man," we can find authoritarian thinkers of a specifically modern cast (e.g., Hobbes) who argue that individuals are self-contained units (here Hobbes and Locke are in basic agreement), fully realized in a state of nature. But because they seek self-interest, individuals in a state of nature are at war with each other. Therefore, they require a policing power that is beyond the reach of individual self-interest but that is not (in this case) the highest expression of civilization—merely a regulator.

There is also a contrary authoritarian notion of "society." Society might be seen not as a form of order but as a form of disorder that requires an authoritarian state to govern it. Put another way, authoritarians might see humans as either naturally harmonious or as naturally at war. Authoritarianism in *Four Theories* sees the state as approximately like society only more so, and in most cases "society" and "state" are interchangeable terms. Obviously, this makes it difficult to conceive of a theory in which society itself is a mess that requires an authoritarian state.

Why didn't the authors pay more attention to the distinction between state and "civil society" that has been central to so much political philosophy? Because, we suppose, they bifurcated the political universe into "individuals" and "groups," corresponding to the opposition between liberty and authority; then all groups—including state and society—were pretty much the same because they were all defined as "other than individuals." This supports a point we made earlier: the vocabulary and premises of *Four Theories* are basically determined by liberalism.

So far, we have seen that authoritarian thinkers might look upon "man" as complete in nature as well as requiring society, might look upon society as naturally at war as well as a high form of order, and might look upon the state as simply a (powerful) policing authority as well as the highest expression of civilization. What about the other authoritarian premises?

Four Theories posits two different authoritarian notions of knowledge. In one, knowledge is discovered or invented; in the other, knowledge is revealed. This second kind of knowledge is implied in the remark that state authority is "sometimes" derived from "divine guidance." The first kind of knowledge can be the knowledge of the scientist *or* of the propagandist (about which more when we talk about truth); the second is the knowledge of the priest or prophet.

We can also easily discern two different notions of truth in authoritarianism as defined by *Four Theories*. One notion, the one emphasized, defines truth as absolute and unchanging. This is the truth of Plato and the Vatican, as well as the truth of empiricists such as Hobbes; it can be the truth of priests or the truth of scientists. But *Four Theories* mentions another authoritarian truth. This one is entirely relative to and dependent upon the interests of the state: "Truth for the German Nazis was 'our truth—truth for us'—in short, that which would advance the interests and solidarity of the German state" (FT 16). Such truth suits the propagandist but not the scientist or priest; such truth is fine for Hitler (*Four Theories* goes on to quote *Mein Kampf*) but not for Hobbes or Plato or the Pope.

We can see that, even in *Four Theories,* there is not one authoritarianism but many authoritarianisms. The multifariousness of authoritarian theory is easily inferred from a simple catalogue of the thinkers, institutions, and movements that *Four Theories* includes: Plato, Niccolò Machiavelli, Thomas Hobbes, Georg W. F. Hegel, Heinrich von Treitschke, Jean-Jacques Rousseau, Thomas Carlyle, Bernard Bosanquet, Benito Mussolini, Adolf Hitler, fascism, communism, Roman Catholicism, the Tudor and Stuart monarchs, and most of the governments of the post–World War II non-Western world. This is a diverse family indeed.

So what was *Four Theories* doing when it outlined authoritarianism as a theory? Well, we would argue that rather than identifying the essence of authoritarianism it was inventing an ideal type of authoritarianism. Put another way, *Four Theories* did not sift through all of history's authoritarians and find the elements they all shared (though it may have implied that it

authoritarian theory is "idealized" version, has no descriptive power

had); rather, it pondered some examples of authoritarianism and invented a pure and fully formed authoritarian theory that would be useful in normative discussions. This authoritarianism certainly does not represent the common ground between Hitler, Stalin, and the Pope, none of whom can qualify as a "textbook" authoritarian and who, moreover, found little common ground among themselves.

In other words, the "authoritarian theory" is not historically descriptive. It does not really explain what human history's authoritarians thought they were up to. But it really does not have to. What it really wants to do is provide a tool for thinking about issues of press freedom and control, and this is a perfectly legitimate goal.

authoritarian theory is no good tool for thinking, either

So is the "authoritarian theory" a good tool for thinking? We can easily name two reasons why it is not. First, because it functions as a kind of straw man. Second, because it does not permit us to understand authoritarian practice.

Why view authoritarianism as a straw man? Considering the historical context, we know that Siebert and his colleagues can't have expected any of their readers to be "authoritarians." Moreover, the authors imply here and there that authoritarianism was a phase that Western governments passed through in adolescence, as it were. (Germany and Italy entered puberty late but passed through it all right; the Soviet Union had developed some

authoritarian as primitive & instinctive

curious form of deviance.) So authoritarianism was clearly presented as a primitive and instinctive notion that mature societies had outgrown in the eighteenth and nineteenth centuries. A brief look at authoritarian premises bears this assessment out. While a reader finds all sorts of notions in the discussion of the authoritarian theory, those that are emphasized are specifically the ones that can be paired with opposites from the "libertarian theory." In other words, *Four Theories* defines authoritarian-

defined in terms of opposites of libertarianism

ism as the opposite of libertarianism. What better way to make a straw man?

We also remarked that the authoritarian theory is a bad tool for thinking because it does not allow us to understand authoritarian practices. Recall how earlier we noted that anyone who believed in the authoritarian theory would advocate state control of communications. But suppose we ask that question backwards: Does advocating state control require belief in the authoritarian theory? Does censorship, for instance, require a belief that "only through unity could the state operate successfully"? The answer is clearly no, since all sorts of individuals and states that claim adherence to other principles regulate public communications in all sorts of ways and justify that regulation in all sorts of ways. Which of these practices are authoritarian? Is, for instance, the U.S. Federal Communications Act authoritarian? What about restrictions on pornography? Defamation? Military secrets? We can call none of these state practices authoritarian unless we can show that they require as justification, or spring from an adherence to, the authoritarian theory. So the authoritarian theory is a bad tool for thinking because it does not allow us to identify authoritarian practices in liberal states.

It also prohibits us from identifying as authoritarian any entity but the state. In Anglo-American history, of course, liberty was identified with those rights that citizens had to defend from the sovereign. Thus, in Western liberalism generally, freedom was identified with the realm of the individual and power was identified with the state. Since the authoritarian theory is basically the libertarian theory upside-down, the same division of labor is evident: the people act freely and the state controls. But even liberal thinkers such as James Madison, Alexis de Tocqueville, and John Stuart Mill had, by the nineteenth century, begun to think that maybe it was not the state that controlled thought and expression anymore but the mass of citizens all acting as individuals. Moreover, in the liberal economics of Adam Smith, private monopolies threatened free markets as profoundly as state intervention. Why not call these kinds of control authoritarian?

It is probably better to think of authoritarianism as practice rather than as theory. This solves the problem of trying to find theoretical unity or consensus among so many and such different thinkers and movements. It also solves the problem of identifying as authoritarian the activities of liberal states and of forces in civil society. If we say that censorship is an authoritarian practice, for instance, we have no trouble identifying censorship by the British Parliament as authoritarian along with censorship by the Catholic Church or the Legion of Decency or the U.S. Post Office or the British Broadcasting Corporation (BBC).

How would we identify authoritarian practices? A simple rule of thumb suffices. Authoritarian practices should be defined in terms of a concentration of power. The possibility of authoritarianism in communications is present wherever the authority or power exists and is exercised to limit or suppress or define people's thought and expression. Thus, a government censorship agency is obviously authoritarian but a local monopoly newspaper might also be authoritarian. Moreover, authoritarian practices need not be negative in form. An authority may define publication in a positive manner, by producing a flood of publication that effectively drowns alternative publications.

Defining authoritarianism in terms of practices and concentrations of power has another advantage. It permits us to see authoritarianism as a current and probably permanent feature of human society, not something that happened at the dawn of the modern era and then was transcended. And, if the four decades since the publication of *Four Theories* have shown us nothing else, they should have convinced us of this: authoritarianism is not a thing of the past.

The Persistence of Authoritarianism

There is a danger involved in discarding the authoritarian theory as a tool for thinking. By giving up a pretty firm standard for categorization, we risk abandoning the category altogether. The temptation arises of calling all governments authoritarian by nature, since they all involve concentrations of power. Such a move would leave us with no position but anarchism to advocate; no language but utopianism would have political significance. Some of us are prepared to embrace that situation; most of us are not.

There is an even more serious danger in maintaining the authoritarian theory as a standard. If only those governments that embrace authoritarianism as a theory are authoritarian, then very few recent governments can be classified as such. For we would be hard-pressed now to find a government or a constitution that does not proclaim rights, freedom, democracy, and equality.

One of the aftermaths of World War II was the global triumph of liberal rhetoric. Since World War II, almost all governments have claimed to be democracies and to protect the freedoms of their populations. As the former colonies of Europe became the nations of Africa and Asia, they framed their independence and legitimacy in the idiom of the Western Age of Revolution. Many of these states engage in authoritarian practices. But if authoritarianism is understood as a theory, then few of them can really be called authoritarian. Hence the ambivalence of the conclusion to the chapter on authoritarianism in *Four Theories:* "Although the theories themselves have been discarded in most democratic countries, the practices of authoritarian states have tended to influence democratic practices. In some instances they have almost forced libertarian governments to take countersteps which in some aspects are indistinguishable from the totalitarian models" (FT 37). Here authoritarian and libertarian, democratic and totalitarian threaten to converge precisely because authoritarian theory can no longer be credibly expressed in public.[1]

The triumph of liberal rhetoric after World War II did not eliminate authoritarian practices, just as World War I did not make the world safe for democracy. Simultaneously, cold war geopolitics and the exigencies of decolonization drove militarization; in many areas, particularly in Africa and Latin America, militarization merged with both local traditions of autocracy and superpower interests to produce authoritarian regimes. In most cases, these regimes excused themselves without proclaiming a variant of authoritarian theory—they said they were temporary, needed simply for a moment of transition or national emergency, and that they would hold elections and yield power in the near future. In the case of Latin America, such cycles of authoritarianism (*caudillismo*) and democracy date back to the liberation from peninsular rule almost two centuries ago; it is tempting to say that these countries are fated to go on like that forever. Still, many hope that the end of the cold war and the post–World War II triumph of liberal rhetoric (including crusades against racism and sexism) should bring about epochal change. No longer can fear of communist conspiracies justify massive repression. No longer will jealous superpowers coddle dictators—or so we might hope.

But if authoritarian rhetoric has disappeared and authoritarian regimes are disappearing, authoritarian practices are not. Liberal regimes and elements of the private sector are capable of authoritarian practices as well. Moreover, certain elements of contemporary politics and communications lend gravity to calls for authoritarian control.

Even before the end of the cold war, the world was presented with a set of new problems. Some are direct results of the decades of the cold war, such as "ethnic" warfare in the nations of the former Soviet bloc. While generally seen as the natural product of ancient hatreds, such ethnic strife might more usefully be understood as fighting over the really very new apparatus of the nation-state. This is true not only of Eastern Europe but also of Africa and Asia, where what are called tribes or ethnic groups were often brought into existence by the very recent process of nationalization. Whatever the sources of ethnic strife, it is clear that in places as different as Kenya and Serbia the threat of internal war operates as a powerful justification for authoritarian rule. Likewise, cases of religious strife or communal violence in places such as India have been used to justify authoritarian regulation.

There are other sources of collective insecurity in the world. For instance, economic crises will recur, whether because of slow growth (as liberals and conservatives warn) or because of contradictions within capitalism (as Marxists and other critics predict). Economic crises and tensions will continue to be invoked as justifications for regulating political expression nationally and the flow of information internationally. In the same vein, criminality and even ecological crises may provide new sources of collective insecurity. And there are always the irrational sources of insecurity (e.g., fear of the foreigner).

Of course, we have perhaps spoken prematurely of the disappearance of authoritarian rhetoric. The demise of the Soviet bloc leaves the playing field open for a new ideological nemesis, and there are a couple of contenders in the field. One is Islamic fundamentalism, which we are careful to distinguish from Islamic thought generally. Energized by the Iranian Revolution, the resistance to Soviet rule in Afghanistan, and widespread Arab displeasure with the state of Israel, fundamentalism has emerged as a political force in the Middle East as well as in other parts of Africa and Asia. In more than a few cases, "moderate" governments in places such as Egypt have reacted with authoritarian measures against fundamentalism, just as the fundamentalist rulers of Iran have tried to suppress Western secularism. The rise of Islamic fundamentalism has had international repercussions as well—most famously in the Ayatollah Khomeini's *fatwa* or decree of condemnation of the novelist Salman Rushdie for his book *Satanic Verses* (incidentally, mainstream Muslims were quick to condemn the *fatwa*). The Rushdie case is a fascinating example of the rejection of the liberal notion of wordplay. Of course, not all of Islam is fundamentalist, as many of Rushdie's supporters are quick to point out. Likewise, not all fundamentalists are Muslims. Hindu fundamentalism is on the rise in India, and Christian fundamentalism is strong throughout the West. While widely different, all of them share a suspicion of secularism and the particular conceptions of freedom associated with it.

fascism

Fascism is another resurgent authoritarian ideology. Present recently and most dramatically in the reaction to Germany's reunification, fascism has been apparent elsewhere as well—in the revival of the Ku Klux Klan in the United States during the 1980s, in some of the Latin American military regimes of the 1970s and 1980s, and in some youth movements throughout the Western world. While neo-Nazis are not serious contenders for political power yet, they have made enough of an impression, both through political expression and organizing and through extra-legal action, to have prompted good liberals to call for laws that amount to limits to free expression.

So while authoritarianism may seem obsolete, authoritarian practices and regimes remain common, and authoritarian theories and ideologies are quite active.

The Libertarian Theory

Siebert's libertarianism is more concrete and more attractive than his authoritarianism. It is more concrete because of its origins in his study of English history and a canon of liberal thought. It is more sympathetic because, obviously, Siebert prefers it to authoritarianism. And who wouldn't?

But Siebert's libertarianism is a simplification of English history and the canon of liberalism. Astute readers have already noted a slide in our language from libertarian to liberal. We are mindful of the distinction and are concerned to say that liberalism, the broader term, is the appropriate object of study. Libertarianism is a species of liberalism but there are other versions that deserve consideration.

When Siebert constructs his libertarian theory, he cites thinkers from at least three centuries. Most prominently mentioned are John Milton from the seventeenth century, Thomas Jefferson from the eighteenth, and John Stuart Mill from the nineteenth. While all three are part of a (broadly conceived) liberal tradition, none of them is a "textbook" libertarian (though Mill is often taken for such in *On Liberty*). In Siebert's rendering, the distinctions among these fellows are neglected; rather, each is presented as making an incremental contribution to the eventual construction of libertarianism. This approach works some violence on each thinker. Each one inhabited a full mental world, of course, and his thought can be understood properly only in the context of that world. In reconstructing these lost mental worlds, we can see that the canon of liberalism contains several distinct notions of the media and the public sphere, some of which look exotic if not alarming to libertarians.

3 main contributors are taken out of their historical context

The Invention of a Marketplace of Ideas

There have been several distinct conceptions of the public sphere in early modern and modern Western thought. The one most commonly associated with libertarian thought in *Four Theories* and elsewhere is the marketplace of ideas. But there are other conceptions, some quite at odds with marketplace notions. Especially important in the canon of liberalism are two variants, antinomianism and republicanism. Milton's *Areopagitica* is an antinomian text and not at all comfortable with the marketplace. The revolutionary generation in the United States, especially Thomas Jefferson, followed republican conceptions of the public sphere and were likewise suspicious of the marketplace. Neither Milton nor Jefferson can be classified as a marketplace libertarian regarding issues of freedom of expression.

cited contributors do not provide bases for marketplace of ideas

The notion of the marketplace of ideas is central to libertarianism's model of political communication. In the libertarian public sphere, interested parties are supposed to advance interested arguments for their positions, and rational individuals are supposed to choose from among the competing arguments those that best suit their interests; the outcome will be the adoption, as if directed by an invisible hand, of a position that will promote the common good. The inspiration for this metaphor for public discourse is Adam Smith's account of the economic marketplace.

More than a few scholars have read the "marketplace of ideas" into texts written before the publication of Smith's *The Wealth of Nations* (1776). Usually such a reading involves defining the marketplace concept very broadly. This is the tactic used by Jeffery Smith in *Printers and Press Freedom* (1986). Smith claims that the central doctrine of the marketplace of ideas notion is that truth defeats falsehood, an idea found in *Areopagitica:* "Let her and falsehood grapple; whoever knew truth put to the worse in a free and open encounter?" The problem with Smith's definition is that, while it includes Milton, it excludes any number of more modern libertarians who see truth being beaten by falsehood all the time but are unconcerned because the marketplace produces a balance of interests.

In fact, a concern for truth (rather than interest) may be taken as prima facie evidence that a thinker does *not* adhere to a marketplace notion of public discourse. This does not mean that such a thinker cannot embrace freedom of expression. But it does mean that he or she will embrace a model of freedom that includes some moral limits.

Milton is an especially apt case. John Illo (1972; 1988) and a few others have pointed out for many years that there were pretty strict boundaries to Milton's tolerance. Toward the end of *Areopagitica* Milton explicitly rejects "tolerated Popery, or open superstition," for instance, and recommends public burnings for books that have been shown to be mischievous. Why bother with such tactics if truth will defeat falsehood anyway? Clearly, he fears that some falsehoods are very powerful, at least to some people.

But Milton obviously has different standards for different people. In fact, in *Areopagitica* he outlines at least three different models of media effects and apparently meant them to apply to different sorts of people. The most famous, and the most tolerant, is a "weak effects" model, in which the impact of a book is determined by the reader rather than the author, a view summarized in the scriptural aphorism "To the pure all things

Milton's 3 models of media effects

a) weak effects → readers who are "pure" are not affected by media
b) strong effects → media can have strong effects on some people
c) opinion leaders → influence others by disseminating ideas learnt through media

Authoritarianism and Liberalism / 45

are pure." If this were the only model of media effects, there
would never be any reason to suppress any book. Yet Milton
admits by the end of his argument that some books will prove
mischievous. How?

He also alludes to a "strong effects" model. Books, he says, are
not "dead things" but have a "potency" to them; they are "the
precious life-blood of a master spirit." Some books, then, will exert
great authority over some readers. Of course, a truly virtuous reader will be immune from the effects of a bad book, no matter how
potent; but other readers may need to be protected.

Books, however, do not operate in a vacuum. Milton notes
that the contents of books are spread through networks of personal influence, more or less in a two-step model. In this third
model of media effects, opinion leaders are responsible for shap-
ing the attitudes of dependent secondary audiences. Ordinary
folk, then, need guidance; to modern libertarians, this sounds
akin to censorship.

We are tempted to say that Milton was simply inconsistent.
But these divergent notions of media effectiveness are really quite
consistent if applied within a specific social context. Books have
weak effects on virtuous educated folk (like Milton himself) but
may lead the vicious astray; moreover, the educated vicious may
in turn pervert the uneducated, who, whether virtuous or not
by inclination, will be ill-equipped to resist temptation of the
intellectual variety.

Milton's theories make sense in his historical context

We know Milton was furious in his defense of freedom, then,
but freedom for whom? Clearly, it was freedom for the few, specifically the virtuous educated few. But he cared very deeply for
this freedom and was willing to be perceived as arguing for a
much broader freedom. Whence his sense of urgency? Like the
other Puritan radicals of his day (Hill 1972; 1977), Milton was
antinomian. That is, he felt that the most important thing was
the practice of true religion by those capable of it. But this dung-
heap of a world continually interfered with true religion, not
least through the machinery of the state. A bad state persecut-

ed true religion—Milton and his contemporaries had experienced this under the rule of Charles I, recently overthrown at the time *Areopagitica* was written. A good state could be just as bad, though—a good state could seek to compel true religion. But, to an antinomian, true religion can never be compelled, for compulsion inevitably degrades the religious impulse. So Milton must have freedom for himself, not just from malevolent Charles but also from a benevolent Parliament.

[margin handwritten note: antinomianism requires degree of individual freedom]

Did Milton believe in freedom of expression? Yes, but only if it was exercised in the practice of true religion. Indeed, even in *Areopagitica,* when he calls for freedom above all else, he qualifies freedom with the phrase "according to conscience." He put no stock in freedom to be vicious, nor did he treasure freedom to be stupid. He and his contemporaries had seen their fill of the vicious and the stupid; for a brief time, perhaps, Milton expected England to achieve utopia and abolish vice and stupidity, but his optimism could not have lasted long. And his antinomian belief in freedom would not have called for a state policy of toleration anywhere but in a utopia. Any imperfect society would need the state to stamp out "Popery, and open superstition."

Clearly, Milton did not conceive of public discourse as a marketplace. Rather, he seems to have conceived of it as a church; it is easy to imagine him chasing the money changers out of it. But he had little to say about *political* discourse in *Areopagitica* anyway.

Thomas Jefferson, by contrast, had a great deal to say about politics. While known as the great free-press theorist of the revolutionary generation, Jefferson too never appeared to have conceived of public discourse as a marketplace. Instead, he seemed to think of it as a town meeting. The difference between "town meeting" and "marketplace" metaphors of communications corresponded to the difference between two different languages of politics, which historians call republicanism and liberalism (though in the broad sweep of intellectual history republicanism might be seen as a type of liberalism). Republicanism em-

Republicanism: centrality of civic virtue to ensure survival of republican govmt.

Liberalism: pursuit of self-interest → results in common good, 2/0 in republican govmt.

phasized the centrality of civic virtue on the part of individuals to the survival of republican governments, which historically had been fragile. Liberalism, on the other hand, emphasized the propriety of the pursuit of self-interest on the part of individuals and asserted that the common good, including republican government, would result from each citizen's pursuit of private goals. In this sense, liberalism is quite similar to what Siebert identifies as libertarianism. Republicanism saw an organic unity to society—we might say that the community was a natural creature that took precedence over the individual—while liberalism saw societies as artificial conveniences invented by people for their own individual purposes.

Jefferson was almost certainly a liberal in many ways. Theoretically, he was an advocate of commercial farming; practically, he was a capable partisan politician. But when it came to thinking about the public sphere, Jefferson was unmistakably republican. Nowhere is this more apparent than in his most famous defense of freedom of the press, his letter to Carrington.

In the key section of his letter, Jefferson writes:

> The way to prevent these irregular interpositions of the people is to give them full information of their affairs thro' the channel of the public papers, and to contrive that those papers should penetrate the whole mass of the people. The basis of our governments being the opinion of the people, the very first object should be to keep that right; and were it left to me to decide whether we should have a government without newspapers or newspapers without a government, I should not hesitate a moment to prefer the latter. But I should mean that every man should receive those papers and be capable of reading them. I am convinced that those societies (as the Indians) which live without government enjoy in their mass an infinitely greater degree of happiness than those who live under European governments. Among the former, public opinion is in the place of law, and restrains morals as powerfully as laws ever did anywhere. Among the

equal access for everyone to info

public opinion as moral restraint as effective as laws

latter, under pretence of governing they have divided their nations into two classes, wolves and sheep. I do not exaggerate. This is a true picture of Europe. Cherish therefore the spirit of our people, and keep alive their attention. Do not be too severe upon their errors, but reclaim them by enlightening them. If once they become inattentive to the public affairs, then you and I, and Congress, and Assemblies, judges and governors all become wolves. (1787a)

By public opinion he apparently means a sort of natural consensus that forms when all citizens focus their attention on public affairs. This is not the same model of public opinion that we find in modern survey research—the numerical reckoning of how many lean which way on a specific question, which is at root a secularization of electoral politics—but a republican/primitive notion of a public "common sense," not divided according to interest or class but harmonious, not like the nations of Europe (always the model of corruption for Jefferson) but like the tribes of happy Indians.

But such public opinion does not exist naturally in large nations. Instead, some artificial means is needed to allow public opinion to come into existence and function properly. That instrument is the press.

Thus, Jefferson chooses newspapers over government. But not just any newspapers will do; rather, these newspapers must circulate universally, and they must allow the people to deliberate rationally on public affairs, not just as passive readers but as active citizens, participating at all times, not just at election times. The press was to be universal but transparent, an open and, in that sense, passive medium used by active citizens—more like a telephone system than like modern journalism. Such newspapers, by functioning as a vast town meeting, would make government unnecessary—surely a utopian notion—surely such newspapers did not exist.

Jefferson subsequently was much less enthusiastic about real-life newspapers. These "present only the caricatures of disaffected minds" (Jefferson 1803); their "ordures are rapidly depraving the public taste" (1814); their printers "ravin on the agonies of their victims, as wolves do on the blood of the lamb" (1811). Note the ironic twist of diction: it is the press, not the government, that is depicted as bloodthirsty wolves.

To many, Jefferson's condemnation of the newspapers of his day seems simply inconsistent. But his acidity makes sense if we assume that he truly believed in the "town meeting" model of the mediated public sphere. If so, freedom of the press should be something that belongs to all citizens, much like freedom of speech—a conception that is suggested by the wording of the First Amendment. If freedom of the press is the people's, then partisan printers and other vicious propagandists are stealing the press. In doing so, they are disrupting the great town meeting of public discourse; they are artificially creating and maintaining divisions in the polity; they are perverting public opinion; they are, ultimately, making it impossible for the people to be free. The end result could only be tyranny.

For Jefferson, as for Milton, freedom was conditioned by a sense of social order. Freedom was not a simple good thing. Rather, it was good only in the context of a healthy community of intelligent, independent, and therefore virtuous citizens. Without the virtuous community, freedom was useless, perhaps even evil. Moreover, nothing could pervert the virtuous community more effectively than a flood of lies from interested partisans.

Jefferson's concern with truth and virtue explains the tone of his support for a federal bill of rights. He believed the absence of a bill of rights in the original draft of the Constitution to be a great defect (1787b; 1787c). He based his opposition to the Alien and Sedition Acts on a literal interpretation of the First Amendment: *Congress* shall make no law restricting freedom of the press (1798). But he did not deny the authority of the states to make such laws and in fact explicitly supported state regulation of the press on occasion (Jefferson 1804; Levy 1963). To some this seems contradictory.

But Jefferson felt it proper that the press be expected to promote truth. He condoned occasional prosecutions for falsehood because he considered the Federalist press especially to be in the hire of a selfish aristocratic faction. And indeed such a press *could* do harm in the proper circumstances.

To understand Jefferson's notions of the public sphere, then, we have to suppose a republican rather than a libertarian mentality. But, of course, he was an eclectic—perhaps opportunistic—thinker. In this he stands as a symbol of his times, for the people of the early Republic seem not to have resolved the contradictions between republican and libertarian principles.

The conflict between republican and libertarian political languages climaxed in the United States with the debate over political partisanism in the years following the American Revolution, and it was only in this era that the notion of politics as a marketplace became consensual. Partisanism was difficult to justify in republican terms, but candidates for office and newspaper editorialists continued to use republican rhetoric. The result was an unstable contradiction between rhetoric and practice.

Partisanism introduced habits that were explainable in libertarian language and that lent themselves to description by metaphors other than the town meeting. As partisanism gained acceptance, new metaphors were adopted to describe politics: especially the military and the courtroom. Also invoked with increasing regularity was the metaphor of the marketplace.

The actual phrase "marketplace of ideas" is of relatively recent coinage. It is generally attributed to U.S. Supreme Court Justice Oliver Wendell Holmes, writing in the twentieth century. While the term itself is recent, the concept behind the term was widely used by the 1820s. Still, it is habitual for contemporary scholarship on press freedom to attribute it to much earlier thinkers.

Why was the marketplace concept read back into earlier history? One simple explanation is that people felt the need to create an honorable genealogy for contemporary ideas and practices. In fact, by depicting the earliest Western "liberals" as marketplace thinkers, scholars have helped cement the perception that contemporary attitudes are uniformly in line with marketplace liberalism.

But the older metaphors for public discourse have continued to compel commentary. Recent public opinion surveys show large chunks of the population expressing demands for community accountability on the part of the media (as well as other private businesses). The public may admire the marketplace but they balk at having political questions settled by the same logic that sells cars and soap.

Likewise, concentration in media ownership and operation has made the "free market" language of nineteenth-century libertarianism somewhat inappropriate. Reporters and editors have recognized this. About the time that Holmes is said to have coined the phrase, journalists were developing a nascent sense of professionalism that is fundamentally at odds with free market notions of the public sphere. Journalists have come to think of themselves as the eyes and ears of the people, not as contestants in a competitive marketplace.

We should resist the temptation to see professionalism as a simple return to the venerable republican notion of the public sphere. In the town meeting metaphor, citizens did not need mediating professionals to interpret the world for them, tell them what was important, or map out different opinions for them—these were all things that citizens would do for themselves. But these are precisely the functions of responsible professional journalists, whose conception of the media is properly called neoliberal rather than republican.

The neoliberal conception of politics corresponds to the evolution of the social welfare state. Just as with the experience of the industrial revolution, democratic polities took on more and more responsibilities for the general welfare of the citizenry in the face of what seemed a predatory corporate capitalism, so too do neoliberal concepts of the media require the exercise of great-

er responsibility. This neoliberal revision should not be understood as abandoning the liberal concept of the public sphere so
much as changing the concept of the relationship of the media
to the public sphere. Citizens are still free to compete in the
public sphere but neoliberals assert that this sphere—the marketplace of ideas—is *inside* the *media,* unlike earlier days when
the media were inside the marketplace. As such, the media now
have the power—and therefore the responsibility—to regulate
the marketplace of ideas on behalf of the public; and the public is at the mercy of the media in this regard.

Libertarian and neoliberal conceptions of the media's rights
and responsibilities sound similar but are fundamentally at odds.
Both use the rhetoric of freedom of expression but conceive the
media's role in promoting free expression in different ways.
These alternate conceptions are clearly at war in contemporary
media law.

Libertarianism and Neoliberalism in
First Amendment Law

Neoliberal thinking, which includes social responsibility theory, began to make inroads into legal analysis around the beginning of the twentieth century. Harvard Law School Dean Roscoe
Pound, who has been described as "modern America's foremost
legal scholar" (Wigdor 1974), was one of the first to address
implementation of collective rights and interests in law generally. In a 1911 article, he acknowledged that the law up to that
point had emphasized protection of individual interests. Pound
cited the Bill of Rights to the U.S. Constitution, which includes
the First Amendment, as an example of the concern for individual rights (Pound 1911).

But Pound also proposed that law is a tool for promoting *social* interests and that individual interests were protected only
as a means of promoting those social interests. For example, the
law might protect an individual's interest in reputation. If an

individual is defamed, he or she may remedy the injury by su-
ing the defamer in court. Pound would contend, though, that
the law provides a remedy not so much for the benefit of the
individual as for the sake of the community. If individuals could
not sue in court, they might resort to violence and disturb the
general safety and welfare. So the law protects the individual's
interest in reputation but only because it furthers an important
social interest (Pound 1915). When protection of individual interests would be inconsistent with social interests, then the law
need not protect the individual interests.

Individual interests were not totally denigrated, however, just
subordinated to the public interest. As long as the interests co-
incide, then protecting the individual interest will promote the
public interest. But the point is that the individual right to speak
is contingent on promoting the public interest—when the right
to speech fails to promote the public interest, then the speaker's right fails as well.

Pound's sociological jurisprudence profoundly altered law to
accord with neoliberal principles. But he also influenced another
Harvard law professor, Zechariah Chafee, Jr., who was the "seminal figure in the development of the modern constitutional
defense of free speech" (Graber 1991, 122; Smith 1986). Chafee
was the pivotal figure in introducing neoliberal theory into the
law of speech and press. He did not feel bound by the framers'
libertarian leanings. Consistent with Pound's sociological jurisprudence, Chafee proposed that judges should avoid consideration of "natural rights" favored by libertarians and look instead
to actual social conditions. Categorical rules and precedents
should be followed only when they furthered contemporary social interests; otherwise they should be abandoned. Thus, balancing interests according to their social value was appropriate
(Chafee [1947] 1965; 1941).

Chafee adopted the developing notion of a paramount public interest but shaped it in a particular way. The public interest could have been interpreted to allow absolutely no freedom

for speech beyond what Congress was willing to offer, as Chafee's contemporary Edwin Corwin propounded. In particular, Chafee played a vital part in convincing Justice Holmes to put some teeth into the "clear and present danger" test (Ragan 1971). When "clear and present danger" was used in one of the first free speech cases of the twentieth century, Holmes offered total deference to the government's assessment of the danger posed by the speech (*Schenk v. United States*, 249 U.S. 47). Later that same year, however, he and Justice Louis Brandeis dissented when the majority found a clear and present danger in two leaflets that Holmes characterized as "poor and puny anonymities." It was also in this second case (*Abrams v. United States*, 250 U.S. 616, 630) that Holmes introduced the marketplace of ideas metaphor: "When men have realized that time has upset many fighting faiths, they may come to believe even more than they believe the very foundations of their own conduct that the ultimate good desired is better reached by free trade in ideas— that the best test of truth is the power of the thought to get itself accepted in the competition of the market, and that truth is the only ground upon which their wishes safely can be carried out. That at any rate is the theory of our Constitution." What Holmes's eloquence masks, though, is that, even as he wrote, two theories of freedom were competing for acceptance as the best means of creating the marketplace.

Both libertarian and neoliberal theories embraced marketplace rhetoric. Libertarian theory assumes that each speaker, if only protected from government interference, will contribute to the marketplace, and thus all ideas will be disseminated. Neoliberal theory, however, contemplates that the public interest is the touchstone. It may be the optimum to give many individuals as many opportunities as possible to speak but, as the philosopher Alexander Meiklejohn noted, it is essential "not that everyone shall speak, but that everything worth saying shall be said." Meiklejohn sliced to the core of the public interest principle integral to neoliberal theory when he said that "the point of ultimate interest is not the words of the speakers, but the minds of the hearers" (Meiklejohn 1948, 25).

This public right is often referred to in colloquial as well as legal parlance as a "right to know." Unlike the self-defining individual right, terms such as public interest and public's right to know must be ascertained and weighed in each case. The public interest may be on both sides of the balance, as when the public may have an interest in receiving certain information during a trial that might imperil the public interest in the fair administration of justice. The public may have a right *not* to know. These concepts must be defined, and because of neoliberals' distrust of, if not contempt for, the notion that individual speakers might arrive at the proper balance on their own, they turn ineluctably to government.

Both libertarianism and neoliberalism see the potential for private interference with speech entering the marketplace. But libertarians take a decidedly long-term view of "free trade in ideas" and see government involvement in the marketplace as worse than if truth is impeded in a given case. Leaving it to private parties, including the press, as to what will or will not enter the marketplace is a risk. But to acknowledge the risk, for libertarians, is not to necessitate governmental oversight. Libertarians see freedom of speech as playing a fundamental role in a constitutional scheme that attempts to limit government. In this view, government regulation of speech eliminates a critical check on government.

Freedom of speech is risky but the alternative is paternalism. Libertarians believe that no society that trusts government more than it trusts speakers can consider itself free. As Vincent Blasi (1981, 71) remarks, "No system of political authority premised on the consent of the governed can admit the state to [the role of a suspicious, omnipresent tutor], whatever the behavioral consequences." As Justice Robert H. Jackson wrote in *West Virginia State Board of Education v. Barnette* (319 U.S. 624, 640 [1943]),

True, the task of translating the majestic generalities of the Bill of Rights, conceived as part of the pattern of liberal government in the eighteenth century, into concrete restraints on officials dealing with the problems of the twentieth century, is one to disturb self-confidence. These principles grew in soil which also produced a philosophy that the individual was the center of society, that his [*sic*] liberty was attainable through mere absence of governmental restraints, and that government should be entrusted with few controls and only the mildest supervision over men's affairs.

3 libertarian judicial doctrines

This libertarian principle of freedom from government for private speakers has generated three judicial doctrines: (1) no regulation of content, (2) preference for broad rules of general applicability, and (3) a heavy burden of proof on government.

Neoliberals, on the other hand, are much more receptive to government involvement because they identify the problem as private speakers and those who would interfere with the ideal functioning of the marketplace of ideas. It is abuse by speakers that must be corrected, and government is the logical entity to ensure the proper functioning of the marketplace of ideas. While the conception of the First Amendment's freedoms of speech and press in libertarian theory is akin to that of a "shield," protecting the speaker from government, in neoliberal theory it is a sword. The First Amendment is an offensive weapon, and government is charged to act affirmatively in facilitating the freedom of the public.

3 neoliberal judicial doctrines

Neoliberalism has also generated three doctrines: (1) regulation of content, (2) case-by-case balancing, and (3) a light burden of proof on government or even a shift of the burden to the party opposing government.

The doctrinal rules of each theory in practice are the natural outgrowth of the theories themselves. Libertarians favor no content regulation and broad rules as a means of reducing government discretion and interference and of maximizing the speaker's autonomy and the predictability of freedom's boundaries.

Neoliberals counter that courts actually make choices in each case, even if they are citing a supposed natural right or broad rule, and that government can more likely balance what would best serve society's interests than a self-serving speaker. But to do so, judges must consider what was said or should be said, that is, the content, on a case-by-case basis. Any other course might sacrifice the public interest to the private interest, which neoliberals would consider backward.

The two theories and their doctrinal rules are illustrated in two cases, each involving the same issue but with different outcomes. In the first case, *Red Lion Broadcasting Co. v. Federal Communications Commission* (395 U.S. 367 [1969]), an author invoked the fairness doctrine against a station that had broadcast an attack on him. The fairness doctrine's personal attack rule required stations to allow people who had been attacked on their frequency a chance to respond. The rule also required stations that aired attacks to notify the person attacked and offer time—at no charge—to that person. When a station owned by Red Lion Broadcasting refused to comply, the Supreme Court established a precedent that enthusiastically embraced a neoliberal interpretation of the broadcasters' right.

The *Red Lion* opinion is replete with observations that libertarians find almost obsequious in their deference to Congress and the Federal Communications Commission (FCC). After noting that Congress had enacted a law requiring stations that provide air time to political candidates to provide time to their opponents, the author of the unanimous opinion, Justice Byron White, wrote: "It would exceed our competence to hold that the Commission is unauthorized by the [Communications Act] to employ a similar device where personal attacks or political editorials are broadcast." A libertarian might have observed that the First Amendment bestowed the requisite "competence" to decide such questions, but White was unreceptive to such an argument: "There is nothing in the First Amendment which prevents the Government from requiring a licensee to share his [*sic*] frequency with others and to conduct himself [*sic*] as a proxy or fiduciary with obligations to present those views and voices which are representative of his community and which would otherwise, by necessity, be barred from the airwaves" (394).

In a passage rejecting libertarian interpretations of the First Amendment, White observed: "To condition the granting or renewal of licenses on a willingness to present representative community views on controversial issues is consistent with the ends and purposes of those constitutional provisions forbidding the abridgment of freedom of speech and freedom of the press. Congress need not stand idly by and permit those with licenses to ignore the problems which beset the people or to exclude from the airways anything but their own views of fundamental questions" (394). As support for this latter proposition, White referred to the statute and FCC practices that were at issue in the case! He also said, "cases are to this effect," but he cited none, which may have been due to the fact that no Supreme Court had ever decided the particular question that he was treating as a foregone conclusion.

A single sentence summed up the neoliberal thrust of the case: "It is the right of the viewers and listeners, not the right of the broadcasters, which is paramount" (390). This "crucial" right of the public to receive ideas, White noted, could not be abridged by Congress or the FCC. Although White did not explicitly take this argument to its logical conclusion, it would have been consistent with neoliberal theory to add that if the FCC had *not* implemented an access right on behalf of the public, the First Amendment would have been violated. What to libertarians seems to be unacceptable active governmental involvement in controlling content is consistent with neoliberal theory.

Such an affirmative role for government was implicit in a Florida statute that was strikingly similar to the personal attack rule. The statute, passed in 1913, created a right of reply for political candidates whose character or record had been attacked in a newspaper's columns. The newspaper would have to publish at no charge the candidate's response in as conspicuous a place as the attack, in the same type, of the same length. Violation of the statute constituted a criminal misdemeanor.

The case contesting the constitutionality of this statute, *Miami Herald Publishing Co. v. Tornillo* (418 U.S. 241 [1974]) began with an editorial in the *Miami Herald* (Sept. 20, 1972). Pat Tornillo, Jr., a candidate for the Florida House of Representatives, had criticized his opponent for failing to abide by campaign financing disclosure laws. The *Herald*'s editorial twitted Tornillo for spotlighting illegality when in 1968 Tornillo had led a teachers' strike in the public schools, which was contrary to Florida law at the time. Nine days later, and four days before the primary election, the *Herald* turned up the heat on Tornillo. A second editorial blasted him for his "shakedown statesmanship" and for abiding by "Tornillo's law." The piece concluded: "Give him public office, says Pat, and he will no doubt live by the Golden Rule. Our translation reads that as more gold and more rule" (Sept. 29, 1972).

Tornillo sought access to the *Herald* to defend himself, citing the Florida right-of-reply statute, but the paper refused to honor his claim. Tornillo sued. In a neoliberal opinion reminiscent of the *Red Lion* case, the Florida Supreme Court defined First Amendment rights in terms of the public's "need to know," which it held preeminent during an election campaign. An access right, from the public's perspective, was consistent with the First Amendment goal of furthering self-government, according to the court. If an access right produced "ideas and counterthought," then the public could only benefit. "What some segments of the press seem to lose sight of is that the First Amendment is 'not for the benefit of the press so much as for the benefit of us all,'" the court wrote (287 So. 2d 78 [1973]).

With such a strong endorsement from the Florida court and just five years after *Red Lion,* Tornillo might have been optimistic as he awaited the U.S. Supreme Court's verdict on the Florida statute. In 1974, however, the Court wanted no part of an access right and resoundingly dismissed the Florida statute. Chief Justice Warren Burger, writing for the entire Court, characterized the views of various Court members as "strongly adverse" to any right of access to newspapers. Although he devoted the bulk of the opinion to detailing the arguments in favor of access, he dismissed them in a single sentence. No matter how valid those arguments seemed, he wrote, a remedy involving access that did not depend on the discretion of the publisher necessarily implicated government.

Where the *Red Lion* Court had enthusiastically as well as conclusorily embraced the alleged benefits of a governmentally mandated access right, the *Tornillo* Court in the very same manner rejected them. "Government-enforced right of access inescapably 'dampens the vigor and limits the variety of public debate,'" Burger wrote. He concluded, "The choice of material to go into a newspaper, and the decisions made as to limitations on the size and content of the paper, and treatment of public issues and public officials—whether fair or unfair—constitute the exercise of editorial control and judgment. It has yet to be demonstrated how governmental regulation of this crucial process can be exercised consistent with First Amendment guarantees of a free press" (258).

Many criticized the Court for its sweeping language. Benno Schmidt, Jr. (1976), for instance, would have preferred that the Court had spoken more qualifiedly. He valued editorial autonomy, too, but thought access could be implemented in a limited fashion while still largely preserving editorial autonomy.

The qualifications that commentators such as Schmidt would impose on the *Tornillo* decision highlight the fact that it is a model of libertarian theory, unreserved in its endorsement of private control of content free from governmental intrusion. Its broad rule of "no access, period" apparently was meant to minimize, if not eliminate, exceptions, which is consistent with the libertarian preference for predictability. The words and intent of the opinion seem to make the burden on those proposing an access right insurmountable. The Court even went so far as to say that a command to publish was the same as a command not to publish, thus invoking the doctrine against prior restraint at the core of libertarian theory.

Neoliberal theory expressly imposes responsibilities upon the press. The *Tornillo* Court, however, explicitly rejected the notion of legally mandated responsibility: "A responsible press is an undoubtedly desirable goal, but press responsibility is not mandated by the Constitution and like many other virtues it cannot be legislated." That observation evidences a faith in the press and other private speakers rather than a faith in government. It hinges on a belief that even if diversity suffers in a particular instance, in the long run diversity will be better served without governmental involvement.

While the *Tornillo* Court's acceptance of libertarian principles was obvious and unquestioning, the Court's acceptance of neoliberal principles in *Red Lion* was just as obvious and unquestioning. Yet the *Red Lion* case was not even cited in *Tornillo,* much less distinguished. It was as if the Court was at a loss as to how it could explain why it would reach such inconsistent results in two unanimous opinions involving a right of access to a medium to respond to an attack, or else the Court thought that the differences between print and broadcast media so obviously justified the disparate treatment that no explanation was called for.

Actually, the fact that the media were different might explain why different theories operated in each case, but because of history, not technology. Libertarian theory dominates the law of older media, especially speech and press. The doctrine against prior restraint—government may not stop publication because of content in advance of publication—was not only the first definition of free speech and, under any interpretation, within the intent of the framers of the First Amendment, but it also evolved with and is fundamentally symbolic of libertarian the-

newer law is neoliberal

ory. Likewise, constitutional law regarding taxation of the press is among the oldest and most libertarian. But it is the newer law, regarding commercial speech, news gathering, and the broadcasting at issue in *Red Lion,* that is neoliberal.

neoliberal trends → individual rights are translated into public rights

Being the more recent theory and perhaps representative of the dominant worldview (to use Jay Jensen's style of thinking) regarding rights, government, and the law generally, it may be only a matter of time before neoliberal theory supplants libertarian theory as the prevailing mode of interpreting the First Amendment. Indeed, First Amendment law may be the last bastion of libertarian theory. Neoliberal theory controls or is in ascendancy in most other areas where individual rights once dominated, including tort law, land use, product liability, and general taxation. Trends in public thinking (including a sense that problems are so large that only government with all its resources can address them), a sense of risk aversion, identification of speakers more as corporations than as individuals, and a sense that the law should redress all inequities could all subtly nudge courts toward neoliberal theory when they draft First Amendment opinions. Short-term political developments in the early 1990s seem to herald a return to public invocation of minimal government—a standard libertarian theme—and may indicate that the expansion of neoliberalism has been halted or even reversed, but no long-term change is yet evident in the academy or in jurisprudence.

Judges do not refer to libertarian or neoliberal theories when they write, although they do occasionally cite John Stuart Mill or Alexander Meiklejohn. But they, like everybody else, are influenced by the dominant conception of freedom. Libertarian theory has an eloquent and compelling history in free speech law, but it might be considered radical today to dispute that the public has a right to know, however foreign such a legally enforceable right may have seemed to the framers. The influence of Roscoe Pound and Zechariah Chafee cannot be underestimated.

Recent Innovations in Liberal Theory

While neoliberalism seems to be in the ascendant, libertarianism still survives in recognizable form. Friedrich Hayek (1944; 1973–79), for example, argues for a classical liberalism in which liberty is the highest political end. The political philosopher Robert Nozick (1974; 1993) seeks to roll back the bloated, intrusive contemporary state, insisting on an atomistic liberalism driven by individual initiatives and laissez-faire capitalism. Many are persuaded by them.

Yet, insisting on individual rationality and unfettered competition—as classical liberalism has—seems to beg too many questions in these days of the troubled public sphere. Threats to a common social order have fueled a debate within political theory between two sorts of claimants to the mantle of classical liberalism, which we will call egalitarian and communitarian democracy. It is this struggle to revitalize neoliberalism by the philosophers Richard Rorty and John Rawls, on the one hand, and go beyond it by communitarianism, on the other, that has produced the most important recent innovations in liberal theory.

Communitarians recognize that the Enlightenment age is flickering down, its individual autonomy now transmogrified into narcissism and special interests. The theorists of communitarianism—Carole Pateman, Charles Taylor, Michael Sandel, Michael Walzer, and Alasdair MacIntyre—have sought to reconstruct democratic theory accordingly. They show solidarity with neoliberal egalitarianism over against classical liberal individual autonomy. But they introduce their own version of political philosophy that answers most directly the threatened dissolution of public life in contemporary democracies.

Communitarian democracy contends that a liberal politics of rights rests on unsupportable foundations and should be given up for a politics of the common good. The argument can be summarized this way: The politics of individual rights entails that a process guaranteeing fairness should have priority. But individual identities are actually constituted through a social conception of the good. Therefore, claims to rights and notions of justice cannot exist independently of specific forms of political association (Gutmann 1985). For communitarians, libertarianism's appeal to rights and procedural justice lives on a mistaken assumption: it confuses an aggregate of individual goods with the common good. In a communitarian worldview, moral agents can only ascertain what is worth preserving within specific social situations where human identity is contextualized.

In *Sources of the Self* (1989), Charles Taylor's survey of the history of the concept of selfhood, identity is seen as ultimately tied to moral commitment (Fackler 1992, 4–8). "Who am I?" you ask. I give you my middle name, my mother's name, and my height. "That's not enough," you say. "Who are you?" I add more: age, state of residency, shoe size. You are still unsatisfied, if not frustrated. You will likely continue your questions until I can describe to you what I consider to be of utmost importance. My identity is defined by "commitments which provide the frame . . . within which I . . . try to determine . . . what is good" or obligatory (Taylor 1989, 27). If I cannot do so, if I am disoriented and unable to describe the horizon of my valuing, then you will surmise that I am undergoing a severe identity crisis. Should I succeed, your questioning turns to the implications of the self-concept I have articulated. Thus, Taylor draws an essential link between our selfhood and our moral commitments.

Orientation in moral space is as important to identity as orientation in physical space is to locomotion. Imagine someone disputing the idea that we are spatial beings, contending that our concept of up and down is flawed. That is inconceivable in real life. We take it as a given that spatiality requires an orientation to up and down without exception. Likewise, Taylor argues, a concept of the self requires the moral equivalent of a spatial orientation. Repudiate the need for one—as both libertarian and egalitarian liberals do—and in the same breath you leave behind the realization, shared as commonly as our spatiality, that to be human is to exist in a moral space centered on good rather than rights. When we isolate ourselves from values, we are left with no resources except our own ingenuity or self-indulgence.

Classical liberals and libertarians, however, are not generally immobilized by a personal crisis; they advance moral assertions and they recognize moral space. What they cannot do—and have no interest in doing—is to explain the moral self in a manner that grants it either the degree of freedom or the responsibility that liberalism itself enjoys. In other words, liberals assert that liberalism is good but have no idea why anyone in liberal societies should be good. In Taylor's view, since Tocqueville, democracy's inescapable challenge is to make compelling our shared obligation to the common good. Atomistic and egalitarian liberalism feed off moral resources that cannot be explicated by their own theories.

Communitarianism rejects the Enlightenment's individualistic rationalism and its egalitarian inflection by making the community ontologically and axiologically prior to persons (i.e., prior in existence and in obligation). Communitarians insist that political institutions are no better than the social and anthropological theories they incorporate. Sandel and Taylor believe that political philosophy must account for the nature of the moral subject and that liberals like Rorty and Rawls fail to do so satisfactorily. Rorty misunderstands this when he claims that the moral subject can be "in some sense necessary, non-contingent and prior to any particular experience" (1988, 259–61). In the process of establishing these claims, communitarianism also contradicts the presumption of pragmatists such as Rorty that liberal institutions can survive even if their philosophical justification has collapsed (Sandel 1982, 49). Communitarianism thus poses a potentially radical answer to the impasse of liberalism.

But other philosophers have maintained their faith in liberalism. Richard Rorty is foremost among those who argue that "liberalism can get along without philosophical presuppositions" in an age in which appeals to first foundations are no longer credible. In his terms, fleshing out and justifying liberalism's base in moral or social theory do not have the central importance that communitarians claim. "We can be as indifferent to philosophical disagreements about the nature of the self as Jefferson was to theological differences about the nature of God." In fact, Rorty argues that Jefferson established American liberal politics by making respectable the idea that "politics can be separated from beliefs about matters of ultimate importance" (Rorty 1988, 263, 257).

Rorty's *Contingency, Irony, and Solidarity* (1989) seeks to establish democratic philosophy in a new key. He develops a notion of private autonomy in which the self creates the conditions of freedom and fulfillment by contributing its own vocabulary to the ongoing human experiment. Through a discussion of John Dewey's and Jürgen Habermas's writings, Rorty argues for a society in which liberalism prospers and authoritarianism, in all forms, recedes. Rorty recognizes that on a theoretical level the task is impossible, but the narrative level—the vision of "liberal irony," as he calls it—constitutes our most likely prospect for a sense of hope for the future (Fackler 1992, 1–3; Glasser and Ettema 1993).

Rorty's democratic liberal irony is the free and open marketplace without guarantees. Ironists affirm the process of discovery consistent with the widest possible freedoms for words and ideas. One abandons traditional metaphysics and theology in the search for liberal irony and focuses instead on questions of freedom and personal creativity—politics stands in for metaphysics, stories for abstractions, metaphors for religious fantasies. The liberal ironist concentrates on those questions that help us widen human possibility and reduce the opportunity for cruelty.

Liberal ironists make a virtue out of the very uncertainty that seems to cripple liberalism. Thinkers like Rorty continue to doubt the vocabulary they currently use—words like freedom, creativity, and cruelty seem to imply a foundation in the metaphysics of morals—but they realize that no discourse can finally confirm or dissolve these doubts. Rorty likens the contingency of language to biological evolution: "new forms of life constantly killing off old forms—not to accomplish a higher purpose, but blindly" (Rorty 1989, 16). Ironists do not ask "How can you know that?" The important question is "Why do you talk that way?" If communication has been understood traditionally as expressing something that was already there, ironists see language as making something that never had been dreamed of before. Thus, the ideal society is one in which "ideals can be fulfilled by persuasion rather than force, by reform rather than revolution, by the free and open encounters of present linguistic . . . practices with suggestions for new practices" (Rorty 1989, 60). Together we rehearse our common doubts, affirm our mutual contingencies, and play off the new against the old.

In such a society, there is "no purpose except freedom, no goals except a willingness to see how such encounters go and to abide by the outcome. . . . To see one's language, one's conscience, one's morality, and one's highest hopes as contingent products . . . is to adopt a self-identity which suits one for citizenship in such an ideally liberal state" (Rorty 1989, 61). The agenda for progress is poetic freedom and restraint of coercive power in order that new contingencies may gain a foothold. Solidarity rests not in our common reason, or in any other theoretical source, but simply in fortunate circumstances. Rorty sums up the vision: "I should like to replace both religious and philosophical accounts of a suprahistorical ground or an end-of-history convergence with an historical narrative about the rise of liberal institutions and customs. . . . Such a narrative would clarify the conditions in which the idea of truth as correspondence to reality might gradually be replaced by the idea of truth as what comes to be believed in the course of free and open encounters" (Rorty 1989, 68). Irony and contingency then require no metaphysics of either self or society.

Contributing to that vision of liberalism, John Rawls develops a conception of justice that avoids "claims about the essential nature and identity of persons. . . . As a practical political matter no general moral conception can provide the basis for a public conception of justice in a modern democratic society" (Rawls 1985, 223–25). Rejecting the assumption that human beings "have a natural center that philosophical inquiry can locate and illuminate," Rorty opts for the self "as a historical contingency all the way through." In a view shared with Rawls, he believes humans are "centerless networks of beliefs and desires" whose "vocabularies and opinions are a way of coping with everyday affairs." "Reflective equilibrium is all we need try for; there is no natural order of justification of beliefs, no predestined outline for argument to trace" (Rorty 1988, 271). Philosophers must "decry the very notion of having a view, while avoiding having a view about having views" (Rorty 1979, 379, 356). Seeking deep agreement divides and alienates. It is enough to settle on widely held convictions, such as belief in religious toleration, rejection of slavery, and freedom of speech, then to organize ideas implicit in these beliefs into a coherent conception of justice. Such an effort is not only enough, it is in fact our only real choice, since no platform above history is available by which moral intuitions arising in history can be rendered finally right or wrong.

In contrast to the coreless egalitarian democracy found in Rorty and Rawls, communitarianism assumes Archimedean points around which the social order revolves. Presuming that we are social beings who organize life and provide it with significance (at least on the immediate plane), then our patterns of life in space and time are inherently value-centered. The social order is not just a functional unit but the arena where our moral space is elaborated. A society's values, therefore, are the web of which it is formed. With values understood as the marrow of community existence, the only option available is putting content into the normative, asking what authentic social existence involves, specifying the ends political entities should serve, and articulating how persons can be nurtured and integrated into social units. In Michael Walzer's terms, a communitarian insistence on goods rather than rights entails a radical shift from the individual to the collective: "Goods in the world have shared meanings because [their] conception and creation are social processes" (Walzer 1983, 7).

This constitutive view shifts our political attention away from the conditions of access and choice to the conditions of self-knowledge (Woodward 1993). For egalitarian liberals, democracy can only insure open access to the courts, schools, press, government, religious institutions, and so forth. To them, freedom means freedom to choose. Walzer, however, focuses on the need to foster self-knowledge. Democratic processes are a mechanism for choice and self-expression but making them ends in themselves rather than means to an end creates a centripetal force threatening self-knowledge and ultimately undermining the democratic ideals of freedom and self-fulfillment. Concentrating instead on the conditions that inhibit or promote self-knowledge leads us more decisively to normative extrapolations of those conditions that empower or oppress, enfranchise or marginalize. For communitarians such as Taylor and Walzer, the cornerstone of the political order is not process (which can be equitable and still produce injustice) but a social conception of the good and common understanding of the moral subject.

Both communitarians and liberal ironists embrace enhanced pluralism. Neither view is content with an insipid, melting-pot nationalism; neither advocates the privatistic species of tasteless, uniform pluralism that currently dominates U.S. politics. Egalitarians expect open access and free choice to generate an inclusive, multicultural, cross-class federation of various races and genders. Communitarians use pluralism to mean confessional diversity guaranteeing an array of ideologies, philosophies of life, and beliefs. They are concerned particularly that subcultures not be assimilated into a shallow whole that trivializes serious political issues and matters of moral substance. Communitarians insist that, because contending worldviews are held within a single sociopolitical arena, each is responsible for demonstrating the way it enhances the common good.

Liberal ironists and communitarians have different expectations for the media. In Rorty's inflection—as with classical liberalism—the underlying purpose of the news media is to present evidence on which decisions can be based, to provide a bounteous fare that the audience and readers can mold into a coherent conversation about everyday social and political practice. The news media provide a public forum of open access. Full disclosure enables the citizenry to cope with the rush of affairs. Public information ought to be unencumbered and fulsome.

Communitarians, on the other hand, worry that our culture tends to stifle our deepest selves and overriding values. They offer an alternative understanding of the media's rationale and mission. A moral framework is assumed to be a condition of community. Therefore, social institutions such as education and the press must empower the public sphere by breathing air into the collapsed lungs of the spirit. News cannot be constrained by the political illusion, by a preoccupation with government busyness in Springfield, Illinois, Washington, D.C., or Berlin. Instead, reporting as a genre should nurture our worldviews, celebrate human solidarity, struggle with tragedy, enable us to develop a philosophy of life, and foster a conception of the common good. As Taylor concludes in *The Ethics of Authenticity*, if we remain inarticulate about social ends, we will lose our ability to adjudicate moral disputes and "destroy the conditions for realizing authenticity itself" (Taylor 1991, 29).

In the communitarian model, the goal of reporting is not intelligence but civic transformation. The press has bigger fish to fry than merely improving technology and streamlining performance, important as those may be. The question is its vocational norm. Information atrophies unless it vivifies human needs. In a communitarian worldview, the news media should seek to engender a like-minded philosophy among the public.

A revitalized citizenship shaped by community norms becomes the press's aim—not merely readers and audiences provided with data but morally literate persons. News would then be an agent of community formation.

Multiculturalism and Postmodernism

Both egalitarian and communitarian thinkers may be thought of as neoliberal. They share in broad terms a commitment to what we think of as liberal values—tolerance, diversity, and freedom—even if they reject the postulates of libertarians. But they understand these values in different ways.

They disagree most visibly on the question of whether people are most usefully thought of as individuals. We have already explored some of the philosophical issues involved in the notion of selfhood in the preceding section. The philosophical issues did not come out of a vacuum, of course; historical developments pushed them to the fore, and these historical developments are unlikely to disappear. We can summarize this history in the phrase "cultural pluralism." As many have pointed out (especially, Habermas [1963] 1989; Rawls 1971), libertarian thinking presumed the negation of the private in the sphere of the public. Put another way, all the things that distinguish one citizen from another—race, class, gender, religion—were to be hidden behind a veil in public. Liberal societies would create neutral processes that would guarantee fairness by pretending that such distinctions did not exist. Justice is blind, after all. The norm of negating the private worked reasonably well when politics was confined to those who shared private interests. When the electorate was limited to propertied Christian white males, as it generally was at the time of the American Revolution, any member of that electorate could believe that his private interests would be protected by guaranteeing individual rights in the public sphere. But they conceived of themselves as free individuals at the expense of the nonfree—slaves, of course, but also women, the poor, and, in many places, the non-Christian.

The limitations to public life were eroded gradually. First religion and property, then race and gender ceased to bar individuals from political participation. But as new groups were enfranchised, they (perhaps inevitably) brought their previously suppressed private concerns into public view. In the words of the feminist slogan, the personal is political—it is a political act to say that what concerns women ought to be kept in the home and out of the Senate. This meant in turn that the newly enfranchised would eventually come to think of themselves as groups and not as individuals. It was easy to be an individual in an age of limits and consensus; it is much harder in a pluralistic social world.

shift from individualistic notion to pluralistic notion

As a result of the broadening of political life, group rights have joined individual rights on the political agenda. This is a dilemma for classical liberals, who cannot really conceive of any unit other than the individual as having rights. Only individuals can speak, own property, make contracts, and so forth. In liberal thinking, collective units exist only as the sum of the individuals that comprise them. Since only persons have rights, corporations must be thought of as fictitious persons in U.S. law.

But the existence of groups in the public sphere is no longer deniable, and the groups have begun to demand rights that make little sense for individuals. They have demanded the right to recognition, the right to be represented as groups in public forums, the right to communicate. These rights are confusing to liberals. To take one familiar example, guaranteeing the right to vote to all African Americans is in no way necessarily related to assuring political representation to them. If a state's electorate is 60 percent white, then that state's legislature can easily be 100 percent white if all the districts are drawn so that each includes a 60 percent white majority. The individual right to vote, which liberals readily endorse, in this case contradicts the

example : individual right to vote w group right of political representation group right to representation. And if we have individual rights in order to protect our interests, then in this case we should not have individual rights because the interests of a whole segment of the population stand in peril.

Generalizing this case means demolishing the liberal understanding of individual rights. Instead of insuring fairness, individual rights insure the perpetuation of systematic disadvantages. Taken to its limit, the argument states that equality of rights insures inequalities among groups. To insure fairness and to protect the private interests of everyone rather than just the privileged, group rights must be guaranteed as well as individual rights. While few in contemporary politics in Western societies will embrace this conclusion in theory, most reach an accommodation in practice, figuring that if groups are not reasonably happy about their chances for fairness, social stability will not be possible. Thus, pragmatists in both parties in the United States invented the strategy of affirmative action for minority groups, and they did so not because they agreed on a philosophy of group rights but because they agreed that the alternative was an endless spiral of violent unrest.

As Western societies grappled with the rise of the disenfranchised, they also sought to wrestle with the cultural effects of accelerating change. As societies lose the moral consensus that provided their sense of collective identity, they also lose the stability that allowed individuals to maintain a sense of self-identity. Individuals in modern societies are usually thought of as centered, as having inner cores of pure self that they sometimes cloak in social situations but that they never lose. But in postmodern societies individuals are fragmented among many identities and subjectivities, sometimes quite inconsistent with each other. Any individual will put on so many masks that the belief in an unalterable inner core cannot be sustained. The subject becomes de-centered. It was easy to think of centered subjects as having rights, of course; de-centered subjects are a different matter. If what we call self-identity is really a kind of confederation of different subject positions or group identities, then are we not on safer ground if we guarantee fairness to groups—which after all are real—rather than rights to individuals, who no longer seem to be real?

One solution to this problem that remains within the terrain described as neoliberal is communitarianism (discussed in the previous section). But communitarianism is bedeviled by both postmodern and multicultural notions of community. In communitarianism, community means everyone having everything in common; but postmodern and multicultural communities are groups of people having one thing in common. We commonly refer to the "gay community" in designating all homosexuals, for instance, or the "Hispanic community" in designating all native Spanish speakers. These communities are certainly not communities in a communitarian sense but where can we find such communities? Contemporary societies are too vast for any group to encompass; within the greater society, groups conform to the postmodern or multicultural model; any local society—Peoria, Illinois, say—will be fragmented by dozens of competing community interests; and any individual will belong to more communities than we can rightly reckon.

If group rights is the chief problem for liberal political theory in the age of multiculturalism and postmodernism, what solutions are possible? Three likely positions have emerged:

1. Group rights and therefore justice are equivalent to and in fact composed of individual rights. Therefore, the way to promote group rights is to demand individual rights. Many gays, for instance, have argued that all the gay rights agenda demands is the protection of the rights of gays as individuals. This position is easily reconciled with classical liberalism, of course, and views the multicultural or postmodern dilemma as simply muddled thinking; it has a hard time making sense of systemic disadvantages for some groups, however.

2. Group rights are different from and often conflict with individual rights. In many cases, group rights can be guaran-

teed only at the expense of individual rights. This is the thrust of the feminist argument against pornography (MacKinnon 1993; Matsuda 1993) as well as many arguments against tolerating racist speech. The protection of free expression, it is claimed, results in tangible harm to specific groups; the victims, moreover, are already relatively disadvantaged, while the beneficiaries of guarantees of free expression are relatively advantaged. Law and policy should protect those who need protection most—a demand that classical liberals cannot really reconcile with neutral mechanisms (i.e., blind justice).

3. All these rights are fictions; only power is real. The third position, which might seem to evolve naturally from the second (though the two must not be conflated), simply advocates abandoning the long debate about rights. Centuries of mental effort in defining and debating rights have resulted in the nearly complete obfuscation of the real injustices in any society, which come from differential power. Phantom battles over rights will generally be resolved in favor of those in power, since that is precisely what power means. Sometimes the rhetoric of rights that the empowered have enshrined can be used to pry some boon for the disadvantaged, but that is the only good reason to keep it around.

rights are fictitious; what actually matters, is power

Conclusion

liberation theory an oversimplified attempt to reduce all liberal politics to a simple formula

Siebert's libertarianism and authoritarianism both were oversimplifications. His authoritarian theory, we have argued, was but the evil twin of his libertarian theory, a straw man that makes it more difficult to recognize authoritarian practices. His libertarian theory was an unwise attempt to reduce the entire sweep of liberal political thought to a simple formula.

We think it is better to emphasize the diversity of liberal thought. The bulk of this chapter has been devoted to recovering past versions of liberalism—antinomianism and republicanism, for instance—and outlining contemporary variants, such

*liberalism — old authoritarianism republicanism
new neoliberalism, egalitarianism, communitarianism, multiculturalism*

as neoliberalism, egalitarianism, communitarianism, and multiculturalism, all of which share the broad commitment to tolerance, diversity, and freedom from state control that we associate with liberalism while failing to fit Siebert's pinched definition of libertarianism.

Note

1. The concluding sentence seems to be a veiled reference to McCarthyism and the politics of loyalty in the United States. Grammatically, the sentence is difficult because the antecedent of "they" is unclear—is it authoritarian theories, is it the practices of authoritarian states, is it authoritarian states, or is it democratic practices? Any of these could be syntactically correct, yet none of them really makes sense because none of them should be able to force libertarian states to become totalitarian.

3

Social Responsibility
Theory

❖ ❖ ❖

Social responsibility theory is one response to the perceived impasse of classical liberalism in the twentieth century. Coalescing in the report of the Hutchins Commission in 1947, social responsibility theory takes seriously many of the accusations of critics (from both left and right) of a laissez-faire media system. These critics contend that there are tendencies toward monopolization in the media, that the people or the public are inattentive and not concerned with the rights or interests of those unlike themselves, and that commercialization produces a debased culture and a dangerously selfish politics. In response, social responsibility theory proposes that the media take it upon themselves to elevate their standards, providing citizens with the sort of raw material and disinterested guidance they need to govern themselves. It is urgent that the media do this, social responsibility theorists warn, or an enraged public will allow, if not force, the government to take steps to regulate the media.

The media have both repudiated and embraced social responsibility theory. When *A Free and Responsible Press,* the report of the Commission on Freedom of the Press (the official name of the Hutchins Commission), appeared, its elaborate rethinkings of liberal theory were denounced by industry organizations such

[handwritten margin note: derived from critique of classical liberalism]

as the American Newspaper Publishers Association (ANPA) and others as an entering wedge for government control of the media. At the same time, the notion of "responsibility" appealed to the media on a commonsense level, and in the intervening half century, most of the specific recommendations of the Commission have become mainstays of the workplace culture of journalists, who after all have long had an interest in upgrading their public image and professional status.

origins,
merits,
shortcomings
of SRT

This chapter presents a series of arguments about the origins, merits, and shortcomings of social responsibility theory. One argument is that this theory has been adopted in practice (if not in theory) because developments in society, politics, and the media all made it appropriate. This implies that there is really no novelty in the situation—no new idea under the sun, so to speak. Social responsibility theory amounts to a sterile intellectual exercise, on the one hand, and an apparently spontaneous ideological development, on the other.

enabled
by social
developments

But we might argue that there is a serious intellectual battle being fought around the concept of responsibility. In this view, the adoption of social responsibility theory means a radical reconstruction of the relationship between individuals and communities, with a new emphasis on the latter. Social responsibility theory thus represents the triumph of community over the lone individual.

SRT
aligned
with authori-
tarian
regulation

This begs the argument from the liberal perspective that responsibility is just a nice name for authoritarian regulation. In terms of the paradigm of *Four Theories,* social responsibility theory should be seen as aligned with the authoritarian and Soviet communist theories as permutations of collectivism, all quite inimical to liberal thought.

This argument in turn begs a rebuttal from the left. Rather than being a true communitarianism, and rather than posing a serious threat to class and corporate control of the media, social responsibility theory actually endorses the status quo by erecting standards of performance that can make monopoly

SRT endorses status quo

media seem like the voice of the people, even as the media keep the people silent and stupid.

Of course, all of these arguments presuppose a media system with bottlenecks everywhere. Responsibility, after all, can be exercised only by those with some kind of power. We expect the publishers of newspapers with circulations in the hundreds of thousands and the producers of television shows with audiences in the tens of millions to be responsible in a way that we do not require of soapbox orators. But suppose the future is the soapbox? Many claim that that will be the likely outcome of innovations in telecommunications technology—the information superhighway will have no bottleneck. Will responsibility be a thing of the past?

responsibility is claimed from people with power

Finally, the chapter considers the peculiar situation of advertising. Often demonized as the corrupter of media and citizens, the advertising industry has had a long dalliance with responsibility as a concept. But advertising must embrace market liberalism in its content—it will be biased and will try to promote particular behaviors beneficial to particular private interests. Is responsible advertising an oxymoron?

Can advertising be responsible?

Responsibility, Yes; Theory, No?

Social responsibility theory was formulated at a time when the United States was coming to terms with what commentators have called "late capitalism" and, in retrospect, it may have been only a reaction to changing public expectations. Prior to World War II, many of the most prestigious news organizations in the United States had come under the dominance of wealthy media tycoons, such as William Randolph Hearst, Robert R. McCormick, and Henry Luce. These powerful and successful media owners controlled large newspapers, wire services, radio stations, movie studios, and magazines. They were politically active and used their positions to support candidates and influence elections and legislative action. At the same time, the fed-

origin: before WW II, US dominated by politically influential media tycoons eral government's power was increasing drastically. President Franklin D. Roosevelt's New Deal dealt with the crises of depression and world war by instituting new programs that both expanded the influence of federal government and altered public attitudes toward government's relationship with the private sector. Roosevelt's liberal spending policies also earned him the animosity of most wealthy media figures, who abhorred big government. Roosevelt, in turn, used their virulent opposition to stir public sympathy for his presidency.

media influence was unpopular

Social responsibility theory was developed just after Roosevelt's death, when influential publishers were unpopular with the public. The public remained suspicious of the press, even though new industry leaders were replacing the older, more politically active ones, the press had been formulating "codes of ethics" for decades (the American Society of Newspaper Editors [ASNE] adopted its "Canons of Journalism" in 1923), and television was becoming the most popular medium in the country.

Hutchin Commission

The story of the Hutchins Commission is a familiar one (Blanchard 1977; McIntyre 1987). It was formed in the midst of World War II when Henry Luce, publisher of *Time* and *Life* magazines, asked his old Yale classmate, Robert Maynard Hutchins, then president of the University of Chicago, to recruit a commission to inquire into the proper function of the media in modern democracies. This issue had become urgent for a number of reasons, including the vigorous atmosphere of press criticism of the past few decades, the outbreak of the war, widespread fears of propaganda and totalitarianism, and the expected rise of a generation of new media technologies in the postwar world. The Commission, which consisted mostly of academics with a connection either to Yale or the University of Chicago, deliberated for four years and interviewed dozens of important figures from the media, government, and the academy before issuing its landmark report in 1947.

The Hutchins Commission worked in the context of national and global social change. The Commission's suggestions, while mirroring the public's distaste for powerful media owners, also seemed to reflect a growing expectation for social change. In fact, this call for change actually took a firmer hold in the years to come. Civil rights demonstrations spread throughout the South in the next decade, and legislative and judicial successes followed. Changes in public attitudes affected African Americans but also touched the lives of many disenchanted groups. In the late 1960s and early 1970s, a spontaneous women's rights movement took aim at male-dominated societal values and norms. American Indians, gays, Hispanics, and other groups, who were oppressed or denied equal opportunities by mainstream society, also sought general public acceptance of their cultures, ideas, and status as equal partners in society and the workplace.

energetic social movements 60's - 70's

By the 1960s, within a decade after the publication of *Four Theories,* media began to reflect new societal standards, not only by opening channels and pages to alternate ideas but by supplementing all-male, white staffs with women and minorities. By their very backgrounds, many of these new journalists seemed to offer fresh perspectives. Since early in the nineteenth century, minority publications had served as voices for their respective communities, but now it was expected that integrated news staffs would bring the minority agenda into the white community, keeping minority issues in front of community leaders and decision makers.

involvement of minorities expected

Media were also alert to the movements of government. The federal government had already exercised some control over broadcast content; later, local governments similarly asserted their rights in bargaining with new cable companies. The fear of censorship repeatedly led Hollywood to display its "responsibility," most recently through the ratings system.

While not responding necessarily to government mandates, newspapers and magazines realized that a new, younger, better educated, post–World War II audience wanted less politically biased news coverage and more interpretive writing. Audiences also looked for publications that reflected a wide spectrum of ideas in the community and the nation. This audience demand could not be ignored. The *Chicago Tribune* is a case in point.

audience better educated, want diversity & less bias

Clayton Kirkpatrick, who eventually succeeded Robert R. Mc-
Cormick as editor of the *Chicago Tribune* (McCormick died in
1955 and Kirkpatrick became editor in 1969), recalled that dras-
tic changes at the historically conservative and politically charged
newspaper had to take place or the *Tribune* would not have survived the 1970s. The *Tribune* and most influential magazines and
newspapers did change, eliminating blatant political bias from
news pages and opening their op-ed columns to various shades
of opinion.

In general, major newspapers and magazines became more
audience oriented. News was more interpretive; consumer, business, and lifestyle news competed with political news for space
in newspapers and magazines. In the 1970s, many newspapers
experimented with consumer advice columns and help hotlines.
Newspaper managers not only allowed publication of a variety
of letters to the editor and opinion or commentary columns but
also instituted daily corrections to set straight published, factual errors. Publishers appointed ombudsmen to hear complaints
from readers. By the last decade of the twentieth century, few
newspapers or magazines arrogantly devoted their energies to
hyping certain political parties or candidates favored by wealthy
media owners and, instead, turned to reader surveys to learn
more about what the community or nation wanted to read.
Conservatives argued that a new, liberal bias dominated the nation's most prestigious media during this new era of news coverage but in fact newspapers and magazines were far more strin-
gent in seeking news and editorial balance than they had been
fifty years earlier.

It would seem on the surface, then, that the social responsibility theory not only existed but that the formulation of such
a concept appeared ever more prescient as each decade passed.
But the question remains: Is this social responsibility theory so
radically different from liberal theory, does it really embody new
concepts, or is it merely an evolutionary descendant of classical
liberal doctrines, not really so new in its purposes and goals?

From the moment the U.S. Constitution was ratified, newspapers never really developed into the public-spirited vehicles envisioned by men like Thomas Jefferson. They were often mean-spirited and consumed by political bias but they evolved over the next two centuries to concentrate on news and advertising. The definition and presentation of news also evolved. Fairness and balance coupled with a more objective writing style came to be accepted as the rule, instead of fiery opinion and rhetoric; it is this style that we usually recognize as "responsible journalism." When, then, did the social responsibility theory overtake the libertarian theory? With the era of the mass circulation press? When the rise of advertising made newspapers financially independent of political parties in the late nineteenth century? When Joseph Pulitzer turned the *New York World* into a mass appeal, working-class paper in the 1880s? With the sensational revelations of the reformist muckrakers in the early twentieth century? When radio brought news instantly into living rooms in the 1920s? When Roosevelt declared war on influential media owners?

Vestiges of social responsibility can be found all along the way, long before the Hutchins Commission. But who is to say this was social responsibility rather than just good business? Pulitzer earned a fortune by publishing a newspaper devoted to working-class men and women but treated his own working reporters and editors shamefully. While bringing the world into American living rooms, radio maintained editorial neutrality but devoted almost all its airtime to entertainment, thus avoiding controversy and slighting serious presentation of the news. Media came to seem responsible without embracing the totality of social responsibility theory.

The Radical Nature of Responsibility

We might, then, understand social responsibility theory as a limited adjustment in liberalism brought about by perceived business demands. But such a reading neglects any analysis of the ideas and justifications behind this adjustment. In order to assess social responsibility theory's importance, we must take a closer look at the fundamental concepts that intellectually shaped it.

In a seminal essay in 1958, Sir Isaiah Berlin differentiated negative and positive liberty as two streams in democratic political philosophy—two models distinguishing John Locke from Jean-Jacques Rousseau. Berlin observed that liberal politics avoids schizophrenia by a compromise in everyday affairs, placing positive freedom in the service of its negative counterpart: "Perhaps the chief value for liberals of political—positive—rights, of participating in the government, is as a means of protecting what they hold to be an ultimate value, namely individual—negative—liberty" (Berlin [1958] 1969, 165).[1]

Positive freedom is the conceptual axis around which social responsibility revolves. The legal implications of positive freedom were developed by Zechariah Chafee in his two-volume *Government and Mass Communications* (1947). Chafee's contribution to neoliberal jurisprudence was considered in the previous chapter; in his emphasis on rights and in his suspicions of government action, Chafee's connections to the liberal tradition are clear. His influence on the Hutchins Commission was balanced by William Ernest Hocking (McIntyre 1987), a philosopher whose reformulations of the concepts of freedom and rights as moral (rather than natural or utilitarian) constituted the philosophical core of the Commission's final report. Chafee's work had more practical impact than Hocking's, especially in First Amendment law, and Chafee prevailed over Hocking in restricting the Commission's endorsement of government intervention to promote responsibility. But Hocking remains the most distinctive and innovative contributor to the Commission's work; he is largely responsible for any element of radical change in the final report.

The logic and rationale of positive freedom are the centerpiece of William Ernest Hocking's foundational book, *Freedom of the Press: A Framework of Principle* (1947). Hocking developed in this volume a definition of freedom distinctive from classical liberalism where (negative) liberty means the absence of arbitrary restraint. In the political theory underlying classical liberalism, individuals possess an inner citadel that is inviolate and, therefore, they must be left alone to pursue those ends each considers right or sacred. To contravene these natural rights, from this perspective, is to violate the self's autonomy.

Liberalism's notion of individualistic, negative liberty has typically been contrasted with social responsibility theory in terms of jurisprudence and governmental policy. These debates over policy, shield laws, Freedom of Information probes, and Supreme Court rulings, however, obscure social responsibility's more critical challenge to defend its view of freedom philosophically. The question is whether positive freedom can be reconstructed in terms of the nature of human being. Hocking developed an intellectually rich notion of positive freedom, though it has been largely ignored. Endless fussing about functional matters such as government intrusion prevents a more fundamental analysis of liberty's character. The vitality of social responsibility at this juncture depends more on conceptually recovering positive freedom than on winning debates over journalistic strategy.

philosophical concept of positive freedom vital for understanding SRT

William Ernest Hocking

Hocking himself believed that negative freedom had gone to seed on the empirical level. In "The Future of Liberalism," a 1935 symposium called by the American Philosophical Association, he exposed its pernicious side in the twentieth century. While Hocking recognized that freedom from coercion has provided a significant constraint against undue government encroachment, he also was concerned that a theory of free expression as an individual right did not resolve certain fundamental

[handwritten margin note top: "negative = individual liberty"]

disagreements that have arisen in Anglo-American history. For instance, on what grounds can defenders of negative liberty motivate citizens to take long-term goals seriously? Presuming *[handwritten margin note: "negative 1. → no future vision"]* that a viable social order cannot merely lurch along from day to day, negative liberty does not inspire us with a durable vision of the future. Hocking also contended that a visceral commitment to negative freedom allows the press as a social institution to be co-opted by instrumentalism and professional privilege. (On the other hand, positive freedom is said by its critics to encourage government interference, though Hocking's *Freedom of the Press* itself never condones political intervention, and the Hutchins Commission report, which reflects Hocking's argumentation, considers the government only as a "residual legatee" of last resort.)

Hocking insisted, to the agreement of the commissioners as a whole, that liberty cannot be distinguished from the conditions of its existence. In his role as the Commission's principal philosopher, Hocking contended that freedom of expression was not an inalienable natural right but an earned moral right. *[handwritten margin note: "liberty is conditioned, requires communal duties"]* Hocking's *Freedom of the Press* is a carefully reasoned argument that liberty—given our status as social beings—is not unconditional but involves the necessity of assuming and performing duties beyond self-interest. While errors are inevitable, wrongdoing cancels the rationale for freedom. Positive freedom is a *[handwritten margin note: "positive 1. as defining humanity"]* defining feature of our humanness but must constantly be etched out of our tendency to serve ourselves rather than use our liberty for the common good.

Freedom of the Press: A Framework of Principle brought into focus two of Hocking's earlier classics, *The Meaning of God in Human Experience* (1912) and *Human Nature and Its Reworking* (1918). Together they provide an ontological basis on which to rest both freedom and responsibility. Rather than a doctrine of individual autonomy, Hocking turns both terms on their head—substituting a communitarian intersubjectivity for individualism, and freedom-to-serve for a protectionist autonomy.

Intersubjectivity is Hocking's label for contending that all persons, as subjects of one divine being, are interrelated by the very fact of their common integration prior to any space-time communication. Through intersubjectivity he makes community the gateway to an understanding of persons. For Hocking, personhood entails a region beyond our individual selves possessed in common with others and sustained by a universal life force. The self, community, and universal humanness are interdependent and cosubstantial. Throughout Hocking's three classics, he argues that the philosophy of the person is basically a philosophy of being. At the highest level, being is fundamentally personal. His last published work is a review of Martin Buber's writing, in which he emphasizes with Buber that finite humans are not discrete in themselves but relational to other beings and to divine Being (Hocking 1964, 45–47).

being to be understood in relation to others

Freedom needs, in Hocking's view, an intellectual home within the nature of being itself. He seeks a formulation in which freedom is compatible with, but not necessarily bound to or defined by, any one particular culture or sociopolitical system. Through the concept of positive freedom he develops a rigorous philosophical context in which responsibility becomes not just an archaic survivor from a prescientific age but a constituent part of a metaphysics of human being. Hocking outlines what might be called an ontology of the rational agent whose socially responsible acts are not mere appearances but prima facie duties as the law and our self-awareness testify. With great subtlety, he thereby frees us from a dilemma inherent in the negative liberty model—does it entail self-abnegation or self-realization? In fact, Hocking is a forerunner of the communitarian challenge: rather than being content with equitable democratic processes per se, he helps establish a conceptual basis for the common good.

responsibility "liberty" in human existence

Hocking's Intellectual Tradition

If we take seriously the history of ideas and culture, has freedom's limited scope ever been successfully contradicted? Even John Stuart Mill accepted restraints, such as forcibly preventing people from crossing a collapsing bridge if no time is left to warn them. Western thought has generally acknowledged that freedom—of speech, for instance—cannot be considered an unconditional right without creating injustices in other areas. Strident claims that human beings are a law unto themselves have always foundered against a more articulate accountable freedom.

A notable example is John Milton, who is typically understood as the prototype libertarian advocating an unfettered marketplace of ideas. His defense of liberty—as we argued in chapter 2—was animated by a concern with liberty of conscience; he made claims based on virtue's prerogatives rather than Lockean natural rights. By entering virtue deeply into freedom's definitional fiber, Milton added permanently to the intellectual agenda. (Only Hocking's preoccupation with the *Areopagitica* while ignoring Milton's political pamphlets as a whole—the mischievous penchant of most press theory historians—prevents him from integrating Milton solidly into his own work three hundred years after Milton [Christians and Fackler 1980].) Responsibility, or something like it, then, has often if not always accompanied liberty in the Western tradition.

Building a theory of freedom is a complicated, multileveled enterprise. But the question of justifying the basis for moral judgments and public policy must be answered in any schema. And the justificatory ground within social responsibility theory as Hocking conceived it is the nature of human being. More than three decades ago, Paul Tillich echoed a similar conclusion: "The roots of the moral imperative, the criteria of its validity, the sources of its contents, the forces of its realization, all this can be elaborated only in terms of an analysis of man's being and universal being. There is no answer in ethics without an explicit or implicit assertion about the nature of being" (1954, 73). The foundation for the strongest possible notion of accountability is the nature of human being itself, compatible with but not necessarily bound to or defined by any one particular culture or sociopolitical system. Thus, he advocates a metaphysics of being in which human life is not merely a constituent part but the epicenter.

Certainly our moral possibilities are grounded in our freedom; actions cease to be moral if humankind is unfree—true enough. The debate revolves around the nature of freedom, not its centrality. Hocking and his circle develop the foundation for a radical positive freedom, accountable freedom, human freedom with responsibility as its integrating center. Graham Haydon (1978, 46) refers to this moral outlook as an "ethics of responsibility," a view of "virtue-responsibility" required of human beings without reference to roles. Advocates of an ethic of responsibility "treat the requirement of responsibility as an ever-present moral demand, necessarily incumbent on any person qua person (or qua moral agent) prior, logically, to particular responsibilities." Thus, obligations to fulfill our task or role duties are not the fundamental element in the moral life that many philosophers suggest. Our obligations receive their significance by virtue of responsible persons taking them seriously when they are working on the job or using their expertise in some direct way.

Even so radical a utilitarian as John Stuart Mill captured a glimmer of the primacy of humanity over our roles: "Men are men before they are lawyers, or physicians, or merchants, or manufacturers; and if you make them capable and sensible men, they will make themselves capable and sensible lawyers or physicians" (1867, 388). Because of the fundamental and abiding character of our being responsible selves first of all, journalists, managers, advertisers, scientists, government workers, teachers, and so forth should operate with a sense of collective responsibility issuing from their humanity. In fact, much of what we mean by enlarging the scope of our accountability entails that our duties as experts become so intertwined with our communal relationships that our thinking and action are inseparably shaped by both our expertise and our basic humanness.

While grounding positive freedom in our unassailable human-ness is the correct move intellectually, it is obvious that the na-ture of the self is itself philosophically problematical at present. Our preoccupation with epistemology in the modern age often blinds us to anthropology's importance and has left us with only minimal vocabulary for analyzing the self. Avoiding the old co-nundrums of natural law and fixed human nature has often been deemed sufficient. But in identifying the problematic subject determined by the power/knowledge structures of late capital-ism, the poststructuralists typify a reawakening concern at present. An explicit philosophy of responsible being, however, refuses to surrender human centeredness to the de-centered sub-ject of postmodernism. To this debate, Hocking speaks with ongoing relevance.

"Positive Freedom" as the "Entering Wedge"

While communitarians welcome "responsibility" and "positive freedom" as an expansion of the realm of liberty, libertarians are wary. In terms of libertarian *thought,* the philosophical under-pinnings of social responsibility theory are indeed radical. But their import in *practice* is really very familiar: "responsibility" must mean accountability; accountability requires state interven-tion; and state intervention, history shows, comes at the expense of liberty as defined by libertarians. Their argument follows.

Social responsibility theory, in one sense, is difficult to criti-cize. Taken at its most benign, who could oppose the goal of an honest, industrious, conscientious press committed to the free flow of all information necessary to self-government? The goal is admirable—but it is also consistent with classical liberal or libertarian theory.

This leads to the first criticism of social responsibility theo-ry: its name. Its authors leave the negative inference that any other theory is socially irresponsible. Libertarian theory did not condone abuse of liberty and it, too, sought to further the public

[handwritten marginalia: responsibility → accountability ↑ state intervention]

[handwritten marginalia: name suggests that other theories are socially irresponsible]

interest. The distinction, though, is one of procedure and presumptions. According to James Madison who crafted what libertarians hold to be their classic statement of principles, the First Amendment: "Some degree of abuse is inseparable from the proper use of everything, and in no instance is this more true than in that of the press. It has accordingly been decided by the practice of the States, that it is better to leave a few of its noxious branches to their luxuriant growth, than, by pruning them away, to injure the vigour of those yielding the proper fruits" ([1787] 1941, 570).

But where a libertarian might expect the public interest to be fulfilled in the long run by emphasizing the private, individual interest in each case (e.g., Wortman 1800, 140–48), a neoliberal (as Jay Jensen [1957, 167] termed those espousing social responsibility theory) looks to the public interest. With its emphasis on a variable public interest and ad hoc analysis, neoliberal theory is decidedly short-term in its approach. "Freedom for the thought that we hate" is more easily defensible if focusing on the individual speaker's freedom from government, in other words, negative liberty (*United States v. Schwimmer*, 279 U.S. 644, 655 [1929, Holmes, dissenting]). But under neoliberal theory the burden is on the speaker in each case to justify freedom for such speech as in the public interest, and that can be a hard sell. Imagine a speaker trying to convince an audience that freedom for speech even though offensive by definition to it is in its best interest.

The fundamental distinction between the two theories regards their contrary attitudes toward speakers and government. According to libertarians, government is the "chief foe of liberty," as Theodore Peterson noted (FT 76), and the government that governs least, governs best. But where libertarians are concerned primarily with abuses by government, neoliberals seem more concerned with abuses by corporations and other nongovernment entities.[2] Roberto Mangabeira Unger notes that, in "postliberal" society, "private organizations are increasingly rec-

difference in perspective: neoliberals perceive nongovernmental entities as the threat to freedom ognized and treated as entities with the kind of power that traditional doctrine viewed as the prerogative of government" (1976, 193). Neoliberals do not share libertarians' skepticism toward government and, instead, concentrate on the power they see exercised by, in the present instance, the mass media and their deficiencies, indeed dangers, in exercising that power. For example, when Peterson listed the themes of twentieth-century criticism of the press, first among them was the criticism that it had "wielded its enormous power for its own ends" (FT 78). Peterson cited the report of the Hutchins Commission as a primary authority for developing and giving impetus to social responsibility theory (FT 75).

The Hutchins Commission based its call for responsibility on what libertarians consider to be an exaggerated sense of the power of the media. In its report, the Commission noted often that continued misuse of press power and freedom would necessitate regulation (1947, 3, 5, 11, 48–51).[3] Regulation was thus the fault of the press, not the government, as a libertarian would contend.

Ideas do have a certain power, but the press rarely has the kind of power ascribed to it. Those critical of press power almost always are guilty of attempting to divert attention from other matters, ignoring other influences, or in essence wishing the press would use its supposed power to support their point of view—an argument about content more than power. As Walter Karp (1983) has pointed out, however, even the press fosters the concept of press power. As long as the press is dependent on advertising for its subsidy, the press is well advised to perpetuate the notion that it is inordinately persuasive. Karp added that it behooves those with real power—the politicians and others who can actually declare war, raise taxes, and imprison or execute wrongdoers—to comply in the myth of press power. Such complicity in perpetuating the myth diverts attention and accountability for their own actions.

Even assuming a considerable power of the press, though,

why should regulation follow? A convincing case can be made that a powerful press is advisable as a check on government. For government to regulate the press would negate the check, not to mention place more power in the government, which clearly is already powerful.

The Commission indicated numerous times that it preferred nonregulation and that governmental involvement posed its own risks for freedom. But its reservations usually accompanied remonstrances that there was no other option if the agencies of mass communication did not live up to their potential on their own (3, 5, 11, 80, 86, 91, 131). The Commission posed self-regulation as a possibility—the ideal even—but at the same time made clear what it saw as the inherent obstacles to that ideal in the nature of competitive, profit-oriented, mass-market media. We are reminded of former Vice President Spiro Agnew's 1969 Des Moines speech in which he expressly repudiated regulation of the broadcast media while the remainder of his remarks on their incredible power seemingly left no other remedy.[4] Was the Commission's rejection of government regulation simply for the sake of "plausible deniability"?

The Commission was in fact ambiguous about the amount of governmental interference it would countenance. It adopted member Harold Lasswell's suggestion that it endorse *both* negative and positive liberty. The former, which is integral to libertarian theory, is associated with the absence of government, "freedom from"; but "freedom for" furthering the public's interest must be facilitated by some entity, presumably government. One view presumes a passive government, the other an active government.

This tension, if not outright contradiction, is treated more candidly in Peterson's summary in *Four Theories,* but the Commission treats the two attitudes toward government as if they were complementary. This blithe conjunction of opposites may say more about the nature of committee work than about theory itself, where different elements must be appeased in the final report. Negative liberty, however, is not what is left over after the government has decided when it must intervene to facilitate the public interest. The government's *failure* to intervene can be a denial of positive liberty.

A speaker exercising negative liberty is free to further his or her own agenda. A speaker exercising positive liberty is free, with the government's assistance, to further the public interest—but opportunities for freedom of speech *not* in the public interest need not be created regardless of the speaker's interest in the speech. In a statement that could well be the credo of neoliberalism, Alexander Meiklejohn wrote that it was essential "not that everyone shall speak, but that everything worth saying shall be said" (1948, 25). Commission member William E. Hocking wrote that censorship was appropriate to prevent "diseducation" from speech that is only of negative worth (1947, 191–93). That is consistent with Meiklejohn's formulation of positive liberty but inconsistent with negative liberty.

The Commission's preference for positive liberty is implicit in the title of its report, *A Free and Responsible Press.* A libertarian might well posit that freedom includes the right to be irresponsible. George Hay, for example, wrote in 1799 that, both before and after the First Amendment, freedom meant "the total exemption of the press from any kind of legislative control" no matter how false or scandalous its expression. For government to regulate expression for the public good, he said, would mean that the First Amendment contemplated not a right but a privilege, a position he called "the grossest absurdity that ever was conceived by the human mind." The press should be liable for "reparation" of individual reputation but essentially should be able to "do whatever it pleases to do, uncontrolled by any law" (Hay [1799] 1970, 34–41).

The Commission acknowledged that any "power capable of protecting freedom is also capable of infringing freedom" (115) and "government has its own peculiar form of temptation to manage ideas and images entering public debate" (116). But in the next passage the Commission declares that the remedy is for government to "set limits" upon itself when tempted (116), a self-restraint of which libertarians would be skeptical.

The Commission noted a "presumption against the use of legal action to curb press abuse" (123) but then questioned the exercise of freedom that does not serve the public interest, adding, "Freedom to express has hitherto included freedom to refrain from expressing; for the press this liberty is no longer perfect" (124). The interest of the public has acquired the "stature of a *right*" (125, emphasis in original) and "protection of the freedom of the issuer is no longer sufficient to protect automatically either the consumer or the community" (125).

Although the Commission emphasized self-regulation, it left the door open for considerable government intrusion. The press, in the Commission's view, had the primary responsibility to define and realize standards of social responsibility but the process should also "be systematically associated with corresponding efforts of community, consumers, and government" (127). Government, the Commission continued, may assist in "making distribution more universal and equable, removing hindrances to the free flow of ideas, reducing confusion and promoting the reality of public debate" (127) and providing new legal remedies for "the more patent abuses of the press" (which the Commission likened to clearing the highways of drunken drivers) (127–28). Finally, government should supplement the press's commentary and news supply. The next sentence is telling of the Commission's faith in government: "In so doing, it may present standards for private emulation" (128). The "new legal remedies" were to be implemented with the "precautions" that the Commission had "emphasized" at some unidentified other points in its report (127).

Although ringing endorsements of press freedom can be found elsewhere, when read in context, the nature of the press's freedom is ultimately in serving the public, according to the Commission. The press has no *moral* right *not* to serve the public interest. The Commission attempted a philosophical distinction between moral rights and legal rights, with Chafee especially insisting that journalists might, for example, not be true to their consciences and might lie without forfeiting the *legal* right to speak (10, 122–23; McIntyre 1987, 145). Like its pronouncements on the inadvisability of government regulation, though, the Commission's attempted distinction between moral and legal rights is ambiguous at best if not contradicted outright elsewhere in the report. We may certainly wonder about the import for *legal* rights of pronouncements such as these: "It becomes an imperative question whether press performance can any longer be left to the unregulated initiative of the issuers," and "protection of the freedom of the issuer is no longer sufficient to protect automatically either the consumer or the community. The general policy of laissez faire in this field must be reconsidered" (125).

negative freedom not sufficient

Thus, when the Commission wrote that the freedom of the press was "essential," the reader soon appreciates that the Commission is not talking about the same freedom that libertarians understand the First Amendment to guarantee. "The notion of rights, costless, unconditional, conferred by the Creator at birth, was a marvelous fighting principle against arbitrary governments and had its historical work to do," but that notion is now "invalid" without a concomitant "condition of duty," the Commission wrote (121).

The Commission cited with approval Hocking's book *Freedom of the Press: A Framework of Principle* (127n), published under the auspices of the Commission. Hocking and Zechariah Chafee, vice chairman of the Commission and as close to a libertarian as the Commission had, were embroiled at one point in a dispute over whether the government ought to punish falsehoods. Chafee prevailed and the final report recommended only compulsory correction of errors. But Hocking's writing and neoliberal philosophy is otherwise sprinkled generously throughout the report. Whole passages are repeated in his own book.

Hocking, as has already been noted, emphasized the rights of communities rather than individuals. "Inseparable from the right of the press to be free has been the right of the people to have a free press," Hocking wrote. "But the public interest has advanced beyond that point; it is now the right of the people to have *an adequate press*" (emphasis in original). And of the two rights, it is the right of the public "which today tends to take precedence in importance" (Hocking 1947, 169).

Hocking also assumed that government, in forwarding the public's right to know, would be benevolent. "The state is, in its nature, the greatest instrument for achieving the common purposes of the human community," he wrote (1947, pp. 188–89). He evinced little or none of the skepticism toward the state characteristic of libertarians. Like other neoliberals, Hocking seemed to think that "state intervention [could] make good every lack of liberty and equality," as Jensen observed (1957, 169–70, 190–91).

But neoliberals might do well to adopt more of the libertarian distrust of government. As John Dewey wrote, "even if we are obliged to abandon permanently the earlier belief that governmental action is by its own momentum hostile to free self-government, we are far from having refuted the evidence of history that officials who have political power will use it arbitrarily" (1939, 60).

Neoliberals, in focusing on the power of the press, seem to overlook the negative aspects of the power of government. Even if libertarian theory is "obsolescent," as Peterson contended, and those "who still speak of freedom of the press as a purely personal right are a diminishing breed, lonely and anachronistic" (FT 103), nevertheless libertarians' fundamental wariness of government should not be disregarded lightly. It was based on centuries of experience, and the framers' concern for the penchant of government to aggressively expand the scope of its influence has only been borne out in the years since 1791.

Indeed, we may wonder why the Commission was so anxious to impose its theory of social responsibility on the press when it might apply with equal if not greater force to government. Government, too, engages in speech. Its meetings, documents, and official pronouncements all constitute speech. If government held itself fully accountable to the public's right to know, we may wonder about the need to hold the press accountable. If government cannot hold itself fully accountable, what reason is there to believe it can hold the press accountable?

Applying neoliberal theory to government speech would seem to compensate largely for any shortcomings involved in applying libertarian theory to private speech. Such an approach would obviate many of the major issues in applying neoliberal theory to the press: the definition of press, whether and to what extent its rights exceed those of the public, and the different treatment accorded rights of news gathering and publication.

Indeed, such an approach might be the only way to reconcile the Commission's resort to both negative and positive freedom. Lee C. Bollinger (1991) has suggested essentially that libertarian theory can apply to the print press and neoliberal theory to the broadcast press, which is another reconciliation of the contradiction in the Commission's report. But such an approach is tied to technology, and a dichotomy in theories based on whether the speaker is or is not government seems to best serve the interests of the public in the short- and long-terms.

While *Four Theories* contemplated more than two theories, a credible argument can be made that there really are only two. They simply differ in the extent to which they arrange the balance between speakers and government. History has occasioned no era when the press has been accorded absolute freedom but there have been plenty of instances of government control. Whether the latter go by the labels of authoritarian theory, Soviet communist theory, or social responsibility theory matters little. The real question is whether and when the balance will swing back to liberty.

Responsibility Endorses Liberalism

To many, this apprehension concerning the Hutchins Commission and the concept of responsibility generally seems altogether misplaced. From a left perspective, for instance, neither the Commission nor subsequent theorists have rejected either a liberal hostility to government, a liberal faith in reason, or a liberal belief in private property. Social responsibility is clearly a species of liberalism, as the label "neoliberal" implies.

First and most important, social responsibility theory does not challenge existing legal rights. It makes a point of leaving the machinery of negative liberty intact, despite the radical implications of Hocking's philosophy; instead, it satisfies itself with claims that the landscape of moral rights is different from that of legal rights. It offers not a clue to the practical implementation of moral rights, other than to rule out any radical means—for instance, creating a right of access, defining the media as common carriers (on the legal side), or insisting on the breakup of monopoly daily newspapers or on subsidies for alternative media. If it is philosophically radical, it is programmatically conservative.

Social responsibility theory retains a liberal notion of healthy public discourse. Essentially, it adheres to the notion of a marketplace of ideas but acknowledges that that marketplace must be represented inside a medium. Put another way, where media previously competed in the marketplace, now the marketplace is contained within the media. Here the libertarian critique misjudges the neoliberal notion of the power of the press. The power of the press does not consist of promoting specific ideas or images; the power of the press is the ability of the major media to be the gatekeepers of the public sphere. This power is presupposed in each of the Commission's "Requirements" (chap. 2) for a responsible press.

Social responsibility theory thus seems to renege on its diag-

dauper of monopoly solved by regulation

nosis of the media's structural problems. It grants that there is a "media monopoly" (in the sense later elaborated by Ben H. Bagdikian [1990]) but aspires to little more than seeing the monopolists behave better. Ultimately it embraces professional autonomy for journalists, which seems like an infringement on the rights of media proprietors, though it also seems to be perfectly functional in terms of media profitability. Professionalism, like responsibility, is a notion so commonly accepted that it seems impossible to criticize—who wants their journalists, much less their doctors and teachers, to be less professional? But certainly professionalism is a kind of elitism. And while we hope our doctors are more learned medically than we are, we should be uncomfortable with the notion that our journalists are more learned politically than we are. After all, in democratic societies, it is the public who should govern; democratic media then should let the people talk to each other rather than just listen to experts.

There is no question that the media have adopted a stance of professionalism in the last half century. This might be looked upon as the triumph of social responsibility theory over liberalism. But can we say that this stance has really fulfilled the expectations of the Hutchins Commission?

Has the Press Become Responsible?

Four Theories outlines the six fundamental tasks of the press as servicing the political system, enlightening the public, serving as a watchdog over government, servicing the economic system, providing entertainment, and maintaining its own self-sufficiency. This applies to both classical liberal and social responsibility press theory, but defenders of the social responsibility theory would argue that the press had been deficient on the first three points and would require that media subjugate serving the economic system to promoting the democratic process and enlightening the public. Have they done this?

It would seem, in retrospect, that perhaps the Hutchins Commission's ideas and the concept of a social responsibility theory were a reflection of the trends of the time and that libertarian underpinnings of American media had been shifting gradually for centuries. Public disenchantment with the personalized media ownership of the 1930s and 1940s and a yearning for a new post–World War II era translated into a different media marketplace but, the point is, it was still a marketplace.

Could contemporary responsibility merely be media owners fulfilling the classical liberal goal of maintaining self-sufficiency and servicing the economic system? Or was this a more idealistic campaign to change the press in the country forever to a more collectivist but socially accountable and multicultural body? Whether these changes constituted a new theory or just a reflection of business people adapting to the times is a matter of interpretation and conjecture, but it seems that social responsibility was not really so far away from libertarian precepts.

SRT very close to libertarian [marginalia]

This begs a further question. Regardless of motivation, are media really more socially responsible now than during the 1940s and 1950s? Though noting that in 1956 the social responsibility theory was still only a theory, the authors referred specifically to those media czars who used the press as vehicles for forcing their own ideological viewpoints on the public and setting their own political agendas. What of media in the 1990s? Though most are no longer dominated by single personalities, today's corporate mentality is hardly more scintillating. By the early 1990s, 99 percent of the nation's newspapers were local monopolies and 88 percent of circulation was controlled by a few large corporations. Similarly, magazines, film, television, radio, and book publishing remained in the hands of a handful of corporate owners. After a flirtation with interpretive and investigative reporting in the 1960s and 1970s, news had become largely colorless and less likely to alienate advertisers through controversy or hard-hitting journalism. The interpretive or investigative reporting that remained was often scandal-oriented and su-

media oligarchy [marginalia]

perficial, especially on television. Profit-oriented media owners avoided controversial stands and cut back drastically on the scope and quality of news coverage.

The press has historically resisted social change and paid more attention to the superficial and sensational than to substance, according to social responsibility theory. Has that changed? Discussion of social change could fill volumes but, generally, studies have found that throughout the civil rights struggle, during the Vietnam War era, and into the struggle for equal opportunity for women, mainstream media were slow to react and even slower to adapt. Do media still sensationalize? While it depends on individual interpretation, any random viewing will reveal that television is filled with entertainment and radio is largely devoted to popular music and entertainment. Television networks have slashed news budgets, reduced news staffs, and replaced public affairs stories with soft features. Newspaper stories today are usually shorter in length and less informative than in the previous three decades. Factoids have replaced interpretation. Front pages, even among some of the nation's largest papers, are dotted frequently with erotica, tidbits about movie stars, and sports stories. Magazines, including news magazines, have turned to entertainment, lifestyle discussions, and trivia at the expense of news coverage. The countertrends—C-Span and talk radio, for instance—provide the information and opinions that the mainstream media neglect but serve mainly enthusiasts and rarely reach an audience large and diverse enough to represent the whole public.

Social responsibility theory also notes that historically critics have complained that media endangered public morals, invaded individuals' privacy without cause, and were dominated by the business class. Again, discussion of public morals is a lengthy topic, but the exploitative emphasis upon violence and sex suggests that media today are no more the guardians against moral turpitude than they ever were, and media preoccupation with the private lives of public figures has climbed steadily since the *press not a particularly good word guardian*

1950s. At the same time, profit has often replaced public responsibility, especially when corporate media owners are located in cities thousands of miles away. Thus, rather than place more emphasis upon the goals of society and "full access to the day's intelligence" as the Hutchins Commission envisioned, the press today has resorted to superficial presentation of the news and replaced substantive information with trivia. Granted, the major media have recently made significant improvements in some areas, such as covering presidential campaigns, but even in such high-stakes situations most media do not interpret as much as they gather meaningless or insignificant facts (did he inhale?) or obsess on polls. Many modern newspapers have avoided controversy by sterilizing the news or by presenting no editorial opinion of their own at all, instead shuffling this task on to the "punditocracy." An increasing number refuse to endorse political candidates.

These are all generalizations and it would be wrong to ignore those remaining exceptional newspapers, magazines, films, television programs, and radio presentations that inspire and inform. But by and large, it is difficult to argue, fifty years after the Hutchins Commission findings and forty years after Peterson's essay on social responsibility theory, that media are more socially responsible. They are just different.

media have changed but not toward social responsibility

The transformation and expansion of the economic marketplace for the media has not translated into an expanding marketplace of ideas. Freedom of the press and freedom of speech have traveled separate paths. We are largely left to speak our minds but it is still the business class who will dictate whether the masses will hear us. Knowing this, it is the public's responsibility to pressure largely monopolistic media to maintain open channels and pages.

This translates to a complex, imperfect process where mass consumption is often confused with the democratic flow of information. We cannot always rely upon public pressure to force media responsibility, especially when ratings or advertising rates are at stake. The danger today is not bias but indifference—on the part of the press and the public. If by human nature we are lazy or disinclined to educate ourselves about current affairs, it still is incumbent upon the press to inform and challenge. When corporate media pander to the lowest common denominator and present bland, superficial, uninspiring news and entertainment, this can be no less destructive than was the presentation of biased, weighted political news and opinion of previous years. The watchdog role of the press is as much threatened by weakness from within as by governmental interference from without.

[handwritten margin note: watchdog function neglected]

Will Technology Make Responsibility Obsolete?

Social responsibility theory was developed to alleviate some of the problems of the mass media technologies of the mid-twentieth century. These were characterized by economies of scale, sometimes to the point of natural monopoly status, which produced huge audiences attending to a few voices. The call for the owners and operators of such technologies—especially network television and monopoly daily newspapers—to be socially responsible was clear and compelling.

[handwritten margin note: technological situation in mid-20th C required SRT]

The new technologies of the late twentieth century may produce a great change in communicative structures. It is possible that scarcity will yield to abundance in communications, that the dominance of a few voices will yield to a great chorus. Such a change would render the responsibilities of the old media redundant and obsolete.

In 1620, Francis Bacon wrote in his *Novum Organum* ([1620] 1955, 537–39) that gunpowder, the compass, and movable type were the three great new inventions. "For these three," he wrote, "have changed the appearance and state of the whole world." Gunpowder had equalized power—eradicating the lines between weak and strong, haves and have-nots. The compass opened access to previously uncharted and untraveled continents, roads, rivers, oceans, and skies. The printing press revolutionized social, religious, and political life—providing access to information for significant numbers of people who previously had been closed off from receiving knowledge.

Fast-forward to the 1990s. We find that Bacon's proposition has retained its currency. The United States, which did not exist in the humanist's day, is considered the world's premier power, significantly because it has the most sophisticated "gunpowder." Advanced radar systems and other digital tracking technologies—the modern world's "compass"—have enabled humankind to journey not only to distant points on the earth but also to vast frontiers in outer space. The digitization of the "printing press"—indeed, its evolution since the 1600s and the complementary growth and expansion of electronic communication technologies—has redefined, reconfigured, and redistributed historical relationships concerning who may or may not, can or cannot create, send, receive, store, and redistribute information.

Since Bacon's age, there have been dramatic changes in both the information technologies and public debate and discussion concerning their uses, purposes, and roles. When *Four Theories* was written, it provided a valuable, although not especially profound or original, perspective that helped to intensify the discussion. A fundamental tenet of *Four Theories* was that the structure and organization of government will influence significantly the role, mission, and ownership of mass media systems operating within a given nation-state. Moreover, *Four Theories* seemed to want to suggest that by changing the mass media's "theory" of operation, we might be able to influence and change government. Despite its apparent shortcomings, *Four Theories* seems accurately to recognize and understand the enormous potential for mass media entities to influence the sociopolitical landscape. Recent history demonstrates this with striking resound.

The modern "information society" (we use this term reluctantly, but it still seems the best capsulization of what is meant when traditional forms of electronic media converge with computation technologies and interconnect with other systems) has rekindled a recurring debate: Are new information technologies a threat to the well-being of the political system or do they contribute to its proper functioning? A favorable early evaluation of new communication technologies can be found in the writings of Lewis Mumford (1934), who foresaw a world where individuals who were geographically distant from their leaders could maintain contact; technology would thus make government more responsive. Others predicted that the impact of technologies would be more authoritarian than democratic. George Orwell, whose fantasies of yesterday are well within the bounds of today's realities, is probably the individual most widely known for having offered a different perspective: "The telescreen received and transmitted simultaneously. Any sound Winston made, above the level of a very low whisper, would be picked up by it. . . . He could be seen as well as heard. There was of course no way to know whether you were being watched at any given moment. How often, or on what system, the Thought Police plugged in on any individual wire was guesswork. It was conceivable that they watched everybody all the time" (1949).

liberation notion of self-regulation

Despite some anxiety over the power of new communication technologies, most proponents seem to align their optimism alongside the central premise of the "invisible hand" notion of classical economics: self-correcting market forces will remedy imbalances in the marketplace. The unresolved question is whether people, when adversely affected by some sociopolitical force, will automatically use information as "power" in the context envisioned by Bacon. There are examples that they will do so. Perhaps the most widely disseminated example is the 1991 beating of Rodney King by several police officers in Los Angeles, eventually touching off one of that city's most serious riots. A private citizen used a new information technology (the portable video camera) not only to call public attention to a "common" unacceptable activity (official misuse of force) but also to suggest the opportunity and potential for ordinary citizens to use communication currency to influence governance.

New information technologies are becoming available at rapidly decreasing costs. Although the well-to-do, educated, and politically experienced traditionally have used various communications systems (e.g., mail, telegraph, telephone) to talk to their elected officials, the lowering of the "toll" to travel along the information pathway is making the same interaction accessible to the poor, politically inexperienced, and (unfortunately, some would say) the uneducated. The question that remains, then, is less whether poor and politically inexperienced people will have access to communication channels but more whether and how they will use those channels.

We also need to turn our attention to the changes occurring in information industries and to explore whether in an economic marketplace free from government regulation those corporations who will distribute information as a "product" or commodity can be expected to promote the broader national interest, even if it may be less in their own economic interest.

Ironically, the very logic that should guarantee universal access to the information highway may be constructing roadblocks to the poor and undereducated. The breakup of AT&T in the 1980s, for instance, was meant to serve the public interest. But each of the new competing companies sees its own best interests in serving the relatively affluent, so that capital investment in new technologies like fiber optics tends to bypass poorer neighborhoods. What does this foreshadow for the state of the modern day democracy? After all, in a democracy, influence should not be a function of money; some citizens have little to spend, yet their rights need to be protected. The expressions "information rich" and "information poor" already have achieved lexical status among communications scholars.

Technologies do not invent or deploy themselves. Whatever the promise of new technologies in the abstract, a number of questions merit closer scrutiny. Who are the architects of the information highway? Who do they represent? What tactics do they use to convince policy makers that their views are best for the nation? Why has the number of information conglomerates grown so rapidly in recent years? What is the impact of that growth? The dilemma that major stakeholders and architects of the information highway face in adopting the strategy of making access universal and affordable—consistent with the ideals of the telephone monopoly model—or of deploying advanced communication facilities only to the most sophisticated users and those who can pay the "market" price has broad implications for the modern democracy.

Perhaps new communications technologies will allow individuals to participate more actively in the marketplace of ideas. The older information technologies placed significant restrictions on who could compete. The traditional theoretical model defined communication as involving five discrete elements: the communicator, or sender of the message; the communicatee, or receiver of the message; the transmitting and receiving devices; the message itself; and the receiver's response (feedback) to the original message. (Other models added varying degrees of sophistication to this general concept, including "noise," "perception," etc.) In general, the information media—and most of them until recently have been "mass" media—have emulated this five-element construct. The newspaper produces a message, the subscriber reads it and, if he or she chooses, offers feedback, either through a letter to the editor or via a cancelled subscription. The scenario has remained generally constant with radio, television, magazines, and other mass media. But new technologies can enhance the potential, opportunities, and capacities for the general public to influence the content, delivery, form, and result of media communication. The end-user citizen may evolve into a powerful producer who not only writes and edits the script but also shoots the film, stars in the movie, edits the film, creates the music, defines the audience, and acts as her or his own critic.

Such technologies would corrode the privileged status of communications professionals. The definition of communication and information on the eve of the twenty-first century rests with the speaker and the audience, not necessarily with the guild of information providers called journalists, editors, and photographers, the wealthy class called publishers, the influential class called "opinion leaders," or the media-created class of icons called celebrities or newsmakers. The theoretical underpinnings of news and information as a professional product also are being tested, challenged, and overturned. New spaces are being added to the public sphere that redefine the "agenda" for news reporting enterprises. Even Bill Clinton and Ross Perot seized the opportunity during the 1992 presidential election to embrace and communicate via "new" information technologies, such as cable's MTV and Larry King's call-in program, neither of which symbolizes "traditional" professional journalism's values. The public, using new information technologies (e.g., databases, fax machines, telephones, electronic bulletin boards, desktop publishing, video cameras and recorders, compact discs, and public access channels on cable television) and existing systems (e.g., radio call-in, pseudoevents to obtain press coverage, and talk-show TV) have increased their currency in the information landscape. (Although it still remains to be seen whether they'll be able to afford the toll to have access to the electronic information highway.)

All of this opens up new opportunities for old styles of politics—especially the formation of interest groups. The quantum leap for new information technologies is their enormous capacity and potential to empower the individual end user wherever she may be and whenever he wants to express an opinion or respond to something else in the marketplace of ideas. It is one thing for the mother of a drunk-driving victim to convene a meeting at her church, synagogue, or mosque and win friends and influence people to join her cause. It becomes both evolutionary and revolutionary, however, when she is able to log on to a personal computer communication network, search a database of individuals with an interest that may overlap with hers, compose and distribute a message to her audience at the precise time she chooses to do so, and not only receive and respond to feedback from others on the system but also participate simultaneously in another "public forum" with a different group of individuals concerning a different subject . . . and also a third, and a fourth, and a fifth . . . indeed, an infinite number of marketplaces of ideas.

While we are tempted to shout "Yes!" and smile broadly about the wonders and awesome powers of newer information technologies, we still hear echoes of the question raised earlier—it is not so much whether people will have the technologies as whether they will use them. People have the vote: they do not use it.

Advertising as a Special Case

Many critics blame advertising for the quality of the major media in Western countries (Baker 1994). Advertising is seen as acting as both an economic and a cultural force: creating economies of scale that drive media concentration, chilling criticism of big business, forcing media to emphasize both audiences that will buy and content that will put audiences in a buying mood. In each of these arguments, advertising is urging the media to be irresponsible.

Advertising did not come up for detailed discussion in *Four Theories.* But certainly it was included by implication in the dictum that one role of the press was to "service the economy." The fact that it is not discussed at length implies that it was a taken-for-granted aspect of "free" media (i.e., media construed under the libertarian theory). Likewise, Peterson implies in his chapter on social responsibility theory that advertising is a force that must be kept in check, in much the same way as the profit-motive of media owners must be kept in check. Does advertising favor the libertarian theory and shun social responsibility? Or is it more complicated than that? We have already noted that responsibility did not necessarily contradict the profit-motive of media owners—in many regards, it was just good business sense. What about advertising?

Advertisers might want to think of themselves as responsible, just as journalists do. But they certainly do not have the same responsibilities as journalists. No advertiser would shrink from an advocacy position—that's the whole point of advertising.

"To explain responsibility to advertising people," the late advertising practitioner/gadfly Howard Gossage (1987, chap. 2) observed, "is like trying to convince an eight-year-old that sexual intercourse is more fun than a chocolate ice-cream cone." Realistically, one assumes that the conventional wisdom of *any* period would support his fatalism. But why? Contemporary advertising practice, domestically and internationally, operates within a framework of both forced and voluntary responsibility that, most practitioners would contend, far exceeds that forced on or embraced by virtually any other facet of the media industries.

much more restricted legally and voluntarily

Indeed, dimensions of voluntary responsibility have been part of the advertising experience throughout this century. Its first significant presence occurred in the Progressive Era when, according to Quentin Schultze, "Progressivism for [businessmen] became an ethos of professionalism; they estimated their self-worth according to the degree to which their occupation displayed the typical characteristics of professionalism, notably ethical codes, licensing or certification requirements, and standardized instruction" (1982, 17).

This ongoing concern with various degrees of professional responsibility can be noted in the history of one of advertising's most prominent and influential trade organizations, the American Association of Advertising Agencies (AAAA). Founded in 1917 with "the dreams of its founding members to unify a ragtag industry," the AAAA celebrated its seventy-fifth anniversary in 1992 and, in its commemorative publication, highlighted many actions that could certainly be construed as embodiments of a philosophy of responsibility beyond that of at least the narrowest of the self-interests of the practitioner entities. Examples (drawn from "The Early Years," *Agency*, Spring 1992, 26–33) include:

- 1917—The Division of Advertising of the Committee of Public Information serves to coordinate World War I campaigns for the Army, Navy, Victory Loans, Victory Bonds, the National War Savings Committee, and the Red Cross. Beyond their explicit goals of persuasion and action on behalf of the war effort, these efforts also, according to the AAAA's own perception, "afforded the newly unified advertising industry a chance to demonstrate the potency of a compelling message, well told."

- 1924—The Standards of Practice for Advertising Agencies is developed, including not only proposed standards of advertising business practices but also a declaration that member agencies should "refrain from preparing or handling any advertising of an untruthful, indecent, or objectionable nature."

- 1941—With the aid of the Association of National Advertisers, the War Advertising Council is established, dealing with many of the same issues and functions as its World War I counterpart.

- 1946—The Association votes to continue the financial underwriting of what had become the postwar Advertising Council, still regarded as advertising's most conspicuous presence of social responsibility with more than $1 billion of advertising time and space donated annually. (This group recently started an effort to challenge racism in the aftermath of the 1992 Los Angeles riots.)

- 1947—The "Monthly Exchange of Opinion on Objectionable Advertising" is created.

- 1960—The Association responds to the television era with a "Special Interpretation of the A.A.A.A. Copy Code with Respect to TV Commercials."

- 1962—A new AAAA "Creative Code" is developed and

subsequently endorsed by many other advertising and media organizations.

- 1966—Plans are developed for the creation of the Advertising Educational Foundation which, among other less self-interested activities, seeks to educate the government, the academy, and the media about the virtues of advertising in the economy and society.
- 1970—The organization issues *Political Campaign Advertising and Advertising Agencies* in an attempt to deal with the many abuses of the increasing use of television in political campaigns. (The bestselling book *The Selling of the President* confirms the increasingly obvious excesses.)
- 1971—AAAA joins other industry groups in establishing the National Advertising Review Board apparatus, without qualification the business's most successful self-regulatory effort (more than 2,800 cases have been handled to date).
- 1973—A Minority Internship Program is established.
- 1974—AAAA adopts revised guidelines for the increasingly prevalent form of comparative advertising.
- 1983—With the Association of National Advertisers, AAAA begins to monitor the television networks to determine if the standards to control advertising "clutter" are being honored.
- 1986—The Association initiates the "Media-Advertising Partnership for a Drug-Free America," eventually securing $1.5 billion in donated advertising time and space over a three-year period. (A $25 million effort to combat functional illiteracy was launched during the same period.)

In addition to the activities of this prominent trade organization, many other policing mechanisms exist. A special 1991 report of *Congressional Quarterly Researcher* observed: "Print ads are typically reviewed by legal departments of agencies and advertisers, and often by technical and scientific staffs. Broadcast networks review storyboards of TV ads before they are produced [and] the editors, owners and publishers of broadcast and print media that carry ads constitute a further set of [voluntary] controls" (Clark 1991, 666). Finally, in the course of normal daily practice myriad advertisers, agencies, media, and individual practitioners involve themselves in varied acts of pro bono work or simple volunteerism (Clark 1991, 659).

 Why, then, with this plethora of self-imposed (albeit often clearly self-interested) activities and advertising's claim to be "the most regulated industry" from federal, state, and local governments, do advertisers bemoan their low public reputation?

In part, of course, advertising, as other institutions, lives within that "master institution" of common sense. And, apparently beyond argument, our contemporary common sense is laced with heavy doses of unfocused cynicism, reflected in idle examples such as polling results showing a marked decline of those regarding "most people as honest," and a *Time* cover story asserting "Lying (Everybody's Doing It, Honest)." From this perspective, advertising shares the zeitgeist, and an examination of advertising history suggests that it may be more prone to critical scrutiny during times of particular economic and/or philosophical upheaval (e.g., the Progressive Era, the Great Depression, the mid-sixties to the mid-seventies). But Gossage's "difficulty in explaining responsibility to advertising people" clearly transcends chronology. Witness the advertising pioneer Bruce Barton's 1927 comment: "If advertising persuades some men to live beyond their means, so does matrimony. If advertising speaks to a thousand in order to influence one, so does the church. If advertising is often garrulous and redundant, so is the United States Senate. We are young and law and medicine and theology are old" (Fox 1985, 108)—but much older now.

In part, advertising's seemingly endless travails in the realms of responsibility may be explained by the very environments within which it functions, as well as its inherent dynamics. For as William Leiss, Stephen Kline, and Sut Jhally observe: "Because it stands at the intersection of industry [marketing practices], communications [the mass media], and group interactions [stereotyping], advertising can come under attack from anyone who is upset about any feature of these three domains" (1986, chap. 12) Thus, the ante for advertising to conduct itself responsibly is raised simply because of where it originates (in marketing practices), how it is delivered (through the mass media), and who it represents in its verbal and nonverbal concoctions (groups and the inevitable stereotyping common to mass communications).

[handwritten margin note: it's an... ...ent vulnerable to do undu... Criticism]

As for its inherent dynamics, these factors seem to have particular explanatory power:

• *Operating from comfortable assumptions about the workings of the market system, advertisers may assume they're performing responsibly while pursuing clearly self-interested ends.* By way of example, Congress passed a landmark law in 1990 requiring television stations to prove they were adequately "serving the educational and informational needs" of young viewers or risk losing their licenses (Waters 1992, 88–89). Two years later a study by a coalition of consumer groups concluded that "the TV industry has devised a conscious strategy of redefining virtually all entertainment programs [e.g., *Bucky O'Hare, Chip 'n Dale Rescue Rangers, Yo, Yogi*] for children as educational and informational." Yet, arguing that the children watch what they want to watch, the head of children's programming at CBS noted, "If broccoli is the only thing on a kid's plate, that doesn't mean he's going to eat it," and "Who's to say what's appropriate for our young? How can you have rules about something that subjective? And with all respect to Peggy Charren,[5] who elected her to represent the values of this nation's parents?" (Waters 1992).

We believe there is a clear message here and throughout countless other examples of advertising practice that are considered "irresponsible" by some yet are regarded as the height of sensitivity by practitioners. That message is this: *The advertising business frequently operates on essentially libertarian assumptions, loosely based on a presumed harmony of self-interests as man-*

ifested through the mechanisms of the relatively unregulated market system. Thus, in the example cited, the advertising parties consider their offering of popular children's programming an appropriate response to market mechanisms, with "responsibility" operationally defined as proof of market acceptance—in other words, the popular programming attracts (read "satisfies") a larger number of children than more "educational" fare.

• *The very nature of the advertising message as a biased form of communication clearly raises the issue as to what constitutes "responsible" market information.* "We must," states the president of the American Association of Advertising Agencies, "do a better job of educating the public and Congress of the value of professional communications [i.e., ads] in the healthcare delivery process." He was responding in part to a widely publicized 1990 study that concluded that 92 percent of 109 full-page ads printed in ten major medical journals failed to meet at least one rule of the Food and Drug Administration's regulations (O'Toole 1992, 24; Danzing 1992, 46).

Ads, by their nature, are selective communication forms and, as such, lend themselves to often disparate interpretations of their proper roles. Consider, for example, three prominent and disparate positions: (1) Ads as communication forms are responsible as they are. We recognize their biases and act accordingly. In addition, we are routinely exposed to a multiplicity of views in a rough approximation of a marketplace of ideas. (2) As easily accessible and potentially influential forms of communication, ads must be required to be more responsible (e.g., as with cigarette warnings) so that consumer-citizens are better informed about their potential choices. (3) The communications marketplace is inadequate. Let ads speak with their biased messages but media should provide *additional* voices of information/persuasion so that the sovereign individual is free to make an informed choice from all available information.

Clearly, views one and three paint a far more flattering picture of the individual as decision maker than the easily duped—

and not easily saved—model of point two. The dimensions of responsibility, then, seem heavily dependent on the perceptions in play.

• *Assignment of responsibility depends in large part on whether one agrees or disagrees with the advertiser's intent.* Is it, for example, responsible for a company to advertise a product that is harmful even *when used as intended?* Such is the case with cigarettes, a product class with an annual advertising and promotion budget in excess of $2 billion. Yet advertisers—in their unabashed self-interests—also encourage us to eat healthier foods, take better care of our bodies, and save our money. Moreover, advertisers—with no clear commercial outcome—also ask us to be more tolerant, more charitable, less abusive, and more activist in a host of humanitarian causes.

These are largely micro-concerns. Yet some hold advertising responsible for larger agendas. Advertising, suggests the AAAA in a series of industry-promoting messages, is nothing less than "another word for freedom of choice." But, critics argue, there are far less attractive lessons being taught as well: impatience, selfishness, superficiality. At the level of day-to-day commercial discourse, or the assumed implicit agenda so relentlessly taught and reinforced in virtually all advertising, there are great difficulties in identifying, much less proscribing, responsible activities.

• *Advertising can be considered responsible or irresponsible depending in part on whether it seeks us or we seek it, and with what message.* There are, of course, advertising forms that are commonly sought by interested parties (e.g., the classifieds, catalogues, directories, electronic shopping networks, grocery store ads, etc). Yet by far the majority of the advertising we encounter is inadvertent—it seeks us rather than vice versa. Not surprisingly, this raises a host of issues dealing with responsibility in such areas as timing, privacy, and frequency, to mention only the most obvious.

The Seagram Company has announced that it will place advertisements only in those portions of seven magazines that "reach drinkers or those likely to drink their brands" (Levin 1992). Arguably, then, ads closely aligned with audience interests are more likely to be welcomed than, say, the relatively intrusive—and often poorly matched in terms of product and audience—messages on television or radio. Indeed, it could be hypothesized that the closer the fit between potential consumer interests and the presence of the product or service advertised, the more likely the advertising messages are to be considered appropriate or responsible. Note also that there is no conscious pulling of the punches on the part of the advertiser here—merely an attempt to communicate as effectively as possible.

To some, of course, the height of advertising irresponsibility occurs when a message is delivered in what is perceived as the wrong environment—for example, a feminine hygiene product advertised on television when a mixed audience is present or, for some, *any* advertising before a motion picture, in a schoolroom, or blocking a particularly scenic view along a highway.

There is an old advertising slogan—"The public is a parade, not a mass meeting"—which suggests the need to repeat a particular message until the desired result is achieved. This particular issue of responsibility beyond narrow self-interest is, predictably, accentuated with the broadcast media, where advertising "clutter" is an issue of lost efficiency for advertisers and irritation for the audience.

It is clear to all that advertisers are seeking consumers more relentlessly than ever before through the mass media as well as other less traditional media forms. To the extent that the match of moment, subject, and interest is not apt, there will certainly be charges of irresponsible acts even though advertisers may also find it in their best interests to accomplish the tight fit. As media forms become more specialized—with ensuing customized content—that ideal may be approached, but advertising's sheer *presence* throughout our waking environments will certainly continue to be a vexing issue of what constitutes "proper" responsibility.

• *The relationship of advertising as a third party with the mass media will constantly raise questions concerning what constitutes responsible activity and arrangement.* As we are well aware, advertising has been a significant third party with the traditional publisher/reader and broadcaster/audience relationship from the middle to late nineteenth century with newspapers, early twentieth century with magazines, mid-1920s with radio, and from the outset with television. The ensuing trade-offs are both causes for boasting (e.g., advertising helps the media to be available less expensively without possible dependence on government subsidy) and magnets for criticism, with such highly charged issues as:

1. *The contention that advertising changes the nature of media coverage.* Sporting events are now routinely scheduled and conducted not for the convenience of athletes or spectators but in compliance with the accepted "rules of the game" to assure the most attractive audience size and composition for advertisers. Special sections on gardening, recreation, home energy consumption, and so on are put together by magazines and newspapers not primarily for the edification of readers but as vehicles for collecting specialized consumers for specialized advertisers. Again, the issues of responsibility cloud when the media purveyors point to sizable audiences as proof of interest, if not acceptance.

2. *The contention that the presence or anticipation of advertising can alter media content.* "When was the last time," a media critic observed, "that you saw a serious investigative piece on the activities of used car dealers in your community?" The implication, of course, is that the presence—or promise—of heavy advertising schedules can compromise journalistic zeal. Several studies, for example, have revealed that "magazines become increasingly reluctant to cover smoking risks as their revenue from cigarette ads rises" (Collins 1992, 41). Or, as Gloria Steinem

celebrated in the first issue of the advertising-free *Ms.*:
"Goodbye to cigarette ads where poems should be. Goodbye to celebrity covers and too little space. Goodbye to
cleaning up language so that *Ms.* advertisers won't be
boycotted by the Moral Majority. In fact, goodbye to the
Moral Majority" (Braden 1992).

3. *The contention that the promise of advertising can affect the
type of media available to us.* Home Box Office (HBO) is
fond of boasting that it is able to produce films on subjects
that commercial networks avoid simply because of expected advertiser indifference if not hostility. Are we not far more
likely to be able to imagine an advertiser-supported magazine with a name (and implied "target audience") like *Self-
Indulgent Jogger* than *Old and Poor?* Advertising-carrying
media, then, are quite likely to be "market" sensitive.

Now, this may or may not produce a socially responsive media landscape, depending on the perception applied. The media, again, can use market mechanisms for proxies of satisfac-
tion and assumed "responsibility," at least to the segments so
favored. Television, it has been observed, reflects demography
far more than democracy, yet almost inevitably those overin-
dulged by the media are also those in the greatest positions of
influence, power, and success in their personal and professional
lives and are hence likely to at least feel comfortable with media stasis.

Yet critics contend that if we rely predominantly on naked
market forces to populate and perpetuate our media environment we are inevitably producing a pecking order of media haves
and have-nots dominated by the power of advertising revenues.
From this perspective, then, it is virtually impossible for advertisers to be considered to be acting responsibly toward needs
beyond their own, as it is their actual or promised revenues,
expected or anticipated in the course of what has become accepted as conventional wisdom in media commerce, that are

providing the lure to the media vehicles that, to the critics, lead to high irresponsibility.

While socially responsible advertising seems like an oxymoron to some, it is a presumed fact of everyday commercial life to many of its practitioners and apologists. Beyond even matters of enlightened self-interest, the advertising business can point to specific practices—some institutionalized and many others ad hoc—that clearly meet any reasonable definition of social responsibility. Moreover, in their daily commercial practices, many advertising practitioners implicitly assume their activities are "responsible" because they are allegedly responsive— to the yea/nay behavior of potential consumers of products and services. And by its very nature as an explicit form of mediated persuasion ("paid propaganda," as Gossage referred to it), advertising will inevitably be considered socially irresponsible depending upon the mix of time, place, subject matter, and intent in a given context.

However irresponsible critics may accuse advertising of being, there is little chance of it disappearing anytime soon. Daniel Boorstin has called advertising "the classic rhetoric of democracy" (1974, 11–12). As such, it seems likely to continue to be as zestful, frustrating, and maddeningly complex as the idea system that spawned, nurtured—and still challenges—it.

Conclusion

The case of advertising highlights the complexity of the concept of socially responsible media. Responsible behavior is the ethical requirement of individuals working within specific sectors of the communications environment, and different occupations may have different standards of responsibility or professionalism. But responsible behavior on the microlevel can exist within a laissez-faire system—in other words, under the libertarian theory in the terms used by *Four Theories*. What about the macrolevel?

It seems an open question whether social responsibility theory makes demands on the macrolevel. Certainly the theory expects some kind of stewardship of media resources on behalf of the public; certainly it expects the media to be educators. But at the same time it avoids detailing structural changes (including government regulation) that would allow performance of these functions.

Thus, we continue to argue among ourselves about the promises and dangers of social responsibility theory. These arguments will continue because of the vagueness that necessarily adheres to a notion used by so many people for so many reasons. But even if we restrict ourselves to a single historical document—in this case, the Hutchins Commission report—it seems that we will fail to come to agreement. This is because the Hutchins Commission tried to make a house big enough for all to fit in. In fact, social responsibility theory seems to contain within it several different theories. We can identify at least three.

First, there is a conservative model. This calls for limited adjustments—"Let's just all try a little harder to be fair"—to forestall more radical proposals. Such a call for socially responsible media is little different from the enlightened libertarianism that characterizes mainstream advertising practices. It expects media to remain primarily market- and profit-driven.

A second, moderate model calls for the profit motive to be severely curtailed but only in the presentation of news and opinion. The moderate position wants a benevolent elite of expert professional journalists to be insulated from the crasser concerns of media owners and thus to be free to serve a public that is, of course, also crass but not as canny as the wealthy and powerful. Thus, a protected community of professionals will allow a larger competitive, individualistic society to operate with a modicum of fairness.

A third, radical model calls for transformation of the greater society itself. Instead of responsible media serving an essentially individualistic, competitive public, they should be engaged in supporting and creating a communitarian public. Indeed, truly responsible media can exist only in the context of real communities, communities conceived of as not just based on geographical proximity or superficial interactions among individuals but as the shared creation of a common life, culture, or identity (Christians, Ferre, and Fackler 1993).

These three models meet the standards and requirements of social responsibility theory. While they seem only marginally compatible with each other, they still share some characteristics, especially on the level of policy. They all hope for change to come from moral behavior rather than government action. They all worry at least a little about the ability of the "free market" to resolve social conflict. And they all decline to demand structural change in media industries—even though the communitarians come close. This is a crucial area where Marxism differs, as the next chapter relates.

Notes

1. Writing as a historical sociologist, Orlando Patterson demonstrates that Western freedom is "a tripartite value," a "chorded triad" with three constituent elements: "personal, sovereignal, and civic freedoms" living in an "often fragile unity" (1991, 3, 5). He recognizes the power of "negative, personal freedom"—that is, "the valorization of personal liberty"—as "the core value of Western culture throughout its history" (xiii, 402), but he finds the binary model of political philosophers such as Isaiah Berlin overwrought, "a nonstarter sociologically" (3). As summarized here, Berlin did not develop "a purely negative meaning" (Patterson 1991, 3) but integrated the two dimensions into a workable unit and, in any case, represented analytically a distinction used by Hocking and others during the mid-twentieth century. In terms of Patterson's sociohistorical typology, Hocking provides an alternative to classical liberal versions of personal freedom by formulating a civic con-

ception of freedom as the foundation of social responsibility theory. In this way, Hocking aids in the struggle against what Patterson calls "the ongoing contradictions in civic freedom" (404–5).

2. "Liberalism . . . considered the established government its greatest enemy" (FT 56).

3. The Commission noted that the "agencies of mass communication are an educational instrument, perhaps the most powerful there is" in presenting and attaining social goals (28). The Commission then devoted a substantial portion of its report to its perception of those agencies' inaccuracies, biases, inaccessibility to the impoverished, capitalistic corruption, and the agencies' penchant for the sensational, trivial, novel, and the "scoop" in attempting to appeal to the largest possible audience (52–68).

4. The theme of Agnew's speech was the power of the media, a power "equal to that of local, state and Federal governments all combined," yet one that the "American people would rightly not tolerate . . . in Government." He mentions the "power" of the broadcast media thirteen times in his speech, concluding that it is time such power was "questioned . . . in the hands of a small and unelected elite." He had demurely suggested earlier, however, that it was not his place to suggest answers to the problem, and he was "not asking for Government censorship or any other kind of censorship."

5. She is head of the watchdog group Action for Children's Television.

4

Marxism

❖ ❖ ❖

Four Theories deals with Marxism in an efficient and unfair manner. Marxism is conflated with Stalinism and then dismissed as a cancerous exaggeration of authoritarianism in Wilbur Schramm's chapter, "The Soviet Communist Theory of the Press." The advantages of this approach are obvious. The Soviet model was the leading outgrowth of Marxist thinking in the world of the 1950s and was certainly the commonsense embodiment of Marxism to readers of *Four Theories* then and subsequently. Moreover, dealing honestly with Marx's own thinking about the media was and is an exceptionally murky undertaking. Nowhere does Marx offer a blueprint of a communist media system, though he certainly would have dismissed the Soviet model as a form of state capitalism; furthermore, when Marx did write about the press, particularly in his early years, he seemed to agree in terms of policies if not in terms of fundamental postulates with many nineteenth-century liberals. Schramm's dissection of Stalinism was then an elegant choice, though not a wise one. It has also left him open to accusations of letting a cold war agenda drive his scholarship.

This chapter takes another look at both the Soviet communist system and at Marxism more generally. We assess the development of the Stalinist model in light of its recent demise. We distinguish the usefulness of Marxism as a critical approach from the merits of the Soviet system of governance by outlining the Marxist critique of liberalism. We then offer some thoughts about alternatives to capitalist or liberal media systems.

Revisiting the Soviet Communist Theory of the Press

Of the four theories, the most difficult to explain and to grasp is the Soviet communist theory of the press. The foundational concepts for the libertarian theory, for instance—free speech and the marketplace of ideas—are relatively simple, though obviously they need to be placed into historical and ideological contexts. Although more complex, the social responsibility theory is essentially a derivation of earlier libertarian ideals with a modern addendum, while authoritarian control is as basic in its underpinnings as civilization itself. To understand fully the Soviet communist theory, however, we must be familiar with nineteenth- and twentieth-century world history, Marxist ideals, Russian and Soviet history, and the weaknesses and strengths of the capitalist system.

In his essay in *Four Theories,* Wilbur Schramm accomplished this task by interpreting both a communist philosophy of the press and the adaptation of such a theory within the Soviet Union of the 1950s. Unfortunately, Schramm's work is obviously dated in both its theoretical application and its historical setting. Time has not only added new perspectives to his thesis but also unveiled a mind-set that we, a generation later, would generally describe as a "cold war mentality." This was particularly obvious in Schramm's comparison of Nazi Germany with the Soviet Union, as he attempted to instill in his readers' minds an image of "red fascism," which was so popular just after the Nazi era and as anti-Soviet hysteria was at its height in the United States.

The entire notion of a Soviet communist theory (rather than a Marxist theory) is at the same time misleading and revealing. After all, the authors of *Four Theories* discuss a worldly classical liberal evolution that begins with the Enlightenment and ends with the peculiarities of twentieth-century mass society. Why a Soviet theory? There were other communist nations in the world and the other three theories did not need a national identity. Schramm, while recognizing a distinction between Marxist ideals and the application of these precepts in the Soviet Union, focused on an amorphous "Soviet communist theory" that supposedly existed at the time but that we would simply summarize, in retrospect, as a Stalinist system. The choice to describe a "Soviet" theory rather than a "Marxist" theory tells us that highlighting the contrast between American and Soviet values was a key goal. It also implies a desire to separate liberal, intellectual acceptance of some Marxist doctrines in the 1950s or earlier from an endorsement of press controls and subjugation of individual rights under the regime of Joseph Stalin.

Therefore, we see the press in the Soviet Union in a different light, not just because there no longer is a Soviet Union but because now we better understand the intellectual climate in which *Four Theories* was written. We will first set forth exactly what mood existed in the 1950s, how the press system in the Soviet Union evolved, and how it was perceived in the United States.

The first communist government came to power in 1918 under V. I. Lenin, who died six years later. A cadre of revolutionaries succeeded Lenin but by 1929 Stalin had assumed single, dictatorial control of the party, army, and nation. Stalin ordered a conversion to government ownership of businesses and property, including the media. This underscores a distinction that *Four Theories* makes between authoritarianism and Soviet communism. The Soviet communist theory of the press calls for government ownership and operation of media, not just government control. It also attaches its theoretical power base to the collectivist goals of the working proletariat, while the authoritarian theory consciously ascribes ultimate press control to a leader or group of leaders. Newspapers, magazines, and radio were used to support Stalin's interpretation of Communist Party doctrines and goals, as Schramm describes in his essay, but communist ideology was perverted to reflect a "cult of personality," or a worship of Stalin as an individual. The communist system thus became a Stalinist system in which the Soviet dictator retained personal control of everything. The press was used not so much to support the revolutionaries' originally outlined goals as to reflect Stalin's desires and personal leadership.

After World War II, the United States and the Soviet Union became the world's two rival leading powers. Fear of communism, which had existed in the United States since the successful Bolshevik Revolution in 1918, became the guiding force behind American foreign policy. Mutual distrust led to a military buildup on both sides as well as a war of propaganda and threats. Stalin died in 1953 and was succeeded by a series of Communist Party chairmen who recanted his excesses and labeled him a national disgrace rather than a cult hero.

Thus, Schramm's 1956 essay came at the height of the cold war, just after Stalin's death when he was about to be censured publicly by his successors. The system of press controls that Schramm described are a Stalinist interpretation of communism. Later Soviet leadership was more benign, though still adamant about press supervision. News media were to support the revolution but each Soviet era redefined the revolution. In the 1920s, Soviet newspapers supported and urged the concept of collectivization and nationalization of property. In the 1930s, radio, books, magazines, and newspapers glorified Stalin and his drive for industrialization. Later, anti-Nazism and then anti-Americanism coupled with militarization were pushed to the forefront. Soviet leaders often used state-controlled television broadcasts or newspaper stories to send messages or warnings to foreign leaders. American journalists could learn more about Soviet intentions by reading between the lines in *Pravda* than by monitoring official Soviet statements.

At the same time, the Soviet bureaucracy grew larger and less efficient over the years. The military buildup, economic pressure from the West, competition with the United States for world leadership, and the distribution of privileges among the relatively small party elite kept most Soviet citizens in abject poverty by Western standards, though the Soviet Union was one of the mightiest military and economic forces in the world. This dichotomy eventually led to a demand for reform. When Mikhail Gorbachev assumed the party chairmanship and finally loosened controls on both the economy and personal expression, however, it was too late and the nearly bankrupt country dissolved into a loose confederation of separate, quasi-capitalist nations.

The Soviet communist era has ended but questions remain about the role of the press in the seventy-three-year experiment. Several things are clear. Schramm was correct on some key points. First, the press, while important, was never the focal point of the Soviet implementation of revolutionary ideas. Rejection of capitalism and attainment of a communist economy and society was always paramount. Until Gorbachev, Soviet leaders never saw the press as a vehicle for reform or change in the country. Media remained tools of national planning, and dissidents were considered enemies of society. Second, government ownership of newspapers, magazines, book publishing, radio stations, and television stations remained a fixed part of the Soviet system, although several civic associations also had publications. Strictly private media ownership was not accepted. Third, a fear of capitalism and its influence guided Soviet attitudes toward free expression. "Press freedom" to Soviet communist leaders and intellectuals translated simply to eventual capitalist ownership and was not seriously considered until late in the history of the Union. Fourth, the optimistic expression of humankind's ability to work together toward a common goal, while disregarding personal liberty and expression even as defined in the Soviet constitution, became cloudier and less connected with reality as the Soviet Union aged. Whether this was due to Soviet leadership or to the loftiness of these aspirations will be discussed later. There are other conclusions about the Soviet press system that may be drawn, which Schramm did not illuminate or could not have known.

Collective national policy, as reflected by the daily press, often required media managers to ignore important social and health problems in the Soviet Union. A nuclear disaster in the interior of the Soviet Union in the 1950s, for instance, went unreported and virtually unknown to the world until the late 1980s, because Soviet leaders did not want the capitalist press to use the disaster as cold war propaganda. Teenage delinquency, alcoholism, anti-Semitism, ethnic strife, and poor health care went unreported and largely uncorrected. The Soviet press did not so much lie on such matters as avoid them.

The press, too, was much influenced by Russian attitudes and cultural values, not just communist ideology. By far the largest ethnic group in the Soviet Union, the Russians historically suffered from a collective inferiority complex. Russia before the revolution had been a backward nation, often scorned by Western Europeans and Americans. Concern over reporting too much of what was occurring in the Soviet Union was often as much related to this national xenophobia as to a clash of ideologies.

Over three generations, the diverse Soviet citizenry learned to get along. Controlled media and a managed economy not only contributed to an overbuilt bureaucracy but also fixed the way the Soviet people viewed their media. They accepted a system of limited expression, so long as they were reasonably comfortable. Under these conditions, new media such as television and the expanding number of media outlets in the Soviet Union were irrelevant to the dissemination of ideas. A deteriorating lifestyle and disillusionment with a growing class of comfortable party bureaucrats combined with an expensive arms race and reduced trade with the West to bring about the end of the Soviet Union, rather than a collective passion for individual rights such as free expression.

What, then, can be said about a communist theory of the press? How will media evolve under the handful of communist governments that still exist in the world? What role did Marxism play in the twentieth-century world information system and what place will it occupy in the twenty-first? Anti-Marxists will make much of the demise of the Soviet Union but, in truth, the Soviet experiment proved a weak test of Marxist doctrine. Stalinist dominance and bureaucratic bungling removed the Soviet system from the theoretic underpinnings of communism. Media were not tools for the proletariat to support the revolution but propaganda vehicles for bureaucrats to protect their power and continually redefine the meaning of the vague, constitutional role of the press.

It is also apparent that a communist press system does not thrive in a capitalist world, especially in a modern information order. Leaders of the remaining communist countries will find that the expression of alternative ideas will much more easily find their way into the information flow, whether by official means or otherwise. Maintaining a closed press system devoted to the single goal of furthering the proletarian revolution and eradicating capitalist influence will be a most difficult task for the future, unless all or nearly all the world's nations adopt such press models.

Clearly, too, the world has changed. Capitalist excesses in most industrialized nations have abated from their nineteenth-century levels, and the ardor for communism among the working classes has shifted away from the exploited proletarian masses in industrialized nations to the victimized peasantry in autocratically ruled Third World nations. This was not what Marx had foreseen. His models were designed around capitalist exploitation of the industrial proletariat. How communist or Marxist philosophy will evolve in a Third World, largely nonindustrialized climate remains an open question.

Industrial nations have adopted some of the designs of socialism while retaining capitalist economies. As a result of the expansion of state provision of schooling, housing, and medical care in the West, Marxism seems to have far less appeal at the end of the twentieth century than at the beginning. More pragmatic leftist philosophies may replace dialectic materialism, as an overcrowded planet attempts to deal with twenty-first-century problems.

Finally, it must be noted that the Soviet experience does seem to affirm the importance of rights to free expression. While a desire for press freedom did not directly bring about the demise of the Soviet Union, limits on the media and on dissent allowed Soviet leaders to pursue ruinous economic and social policies without having to answer to an independent press or system of expression that may have forced change. Reform came only just before total economic collapse and political disintegration. The notion of a collectivist subjugation of individual rights and expression in favor of the vague goal of a withered state and a classless society seems badly frayed, if not outmoded, in light of the collapse of the Soviet Union.

It seems apparent as the twenty-first century approaches and modern media become ever more complex that no societal framework will work well without a marketplace of ideas. In the future, leftist theory may emphasize collectivism but must also allow for free expression as a control for human frailty. While the autocratic attitudes of Stalin and some of his successors destroyed the Soviet experiment, it is logical that any ruler with such power will succumb to temptations of exploiting a vague notion of a classless society and a common, proletarian goal. Whether in a nation dominated by a few capitalist media conglomerates, a so-called communist nation, a socialist order, or a dictatorship, a closed or tightly controlled press system will likely fall victim to the kind of exploitation that Marx so greatly detested. Ignoring the need for free expression and the exchange of ideas in favor of any political or ideological goal will lead only to ruin.

The Marxist Critique of Liberalism

The failure of the Soviet system is widely seen as a vindication of capitalism and liberalism. There is little reason to question the assertions that advanced capitalist economies have outproduced their Soviet-style rivals or that the Western democracies have outperformed their rivals in winning the support of their citizenry. Still, there is reason to question whether this translates into a fair test of Marxism. Leaving aside for the moment the question of a blueprint for communications systems, we must wonder whether Marxist criticisms of liberalism and capitalism have really been answered by the failure of the Soviet model. Even if the Soviet system actually was an embodiment of Marxist prescriptions for the media—a claim that is obviously wrong—its demise would not automatically invalidate the Marxist critique of liberalism and capitalism. To say so would be tantamount to saying that, because Copernicus did not propose Einstein's theory of relativity, his critique of the Ptolemaic geocentric model of the universe was wrong. It is, then, worthwhile to reevaluate Marxism as a critique.

The gist of the Marxist critique is that liberalism is blind to its social and economic assumptions. The rhetoric of "freedom" and "rights" wraps persisting inequalities in an impenetrable mist; liberals could emphasize these abstractions only by ignoring the concrete reality of differential power. By chanting the hymn of rights and freedom, liberals seem to promote equality but actually create the conditions under which inequalities are reproduced and reinforced. When concrete realities are factored in, liberalism collapses under the weight of its own contradictions.

Marxists express this critique in several ways. One way is by telling the history of liberalism as a class ideology. A second way is by pointing out the gaps and contradictions in liberal theory, particularly in the "great books." A third way is to show how the constitutional arrangements of liberal societies, such as the United States, reflect the interests of capital rather than of citizens or the public. There are other forms, but we will consider each of these three versions of the critique, starting with the historical.

Classical liberalism was the political expression of an ascending class that uprooted medievalism and replaced it with a new economic system and ideology. The ascendancy of capitalism and the capitalist class had profound effects that can only be hinted at here. Politics was redefined as this new class wrested control from the aristocracy and devised a form of the state that served to sustain its own interests. In England, the monarchy lost power to Parliament and the Lords lost it to the Commons. In the United States, coalitions of capital refused an hereditary aristocracy on principle and established a state that mirrored the interests of propertied classes.

The new class also restructured the relationship of religion to both the state and the economy. The secular state assumed supremacy over the church, mirroring the new kind of secular economy that was governed by what classical liberals announced as natural laws of the market. The Reformation, which had unlocked large parts of Europe from the Roman Church's control, was also an economic transformation in that it often was nourished by merchants and others who saw benefits in freedom from the Roman Church's teachings. In the Middle Ages, Thomas Aquinas had written that a just price (rather than a market price) was the basis of Christian commerce and reiterated that usury could not be tolerated (Thomas Aquinas [1265–71] 1947, 1513–22). These were effective brakes on capital multiplication and accumulation that had to be overcome before the new economic system could "take off" (to use the words of contemporary development scholars). If the Roman Church would not accommodate such demands, then Protestant sects would, especially those teaching that faith alone (not necessarily deeds) justified salvation. The new rising class unleashed commerce from religious teaching. Economic transactions were secularized and insulated from Christian morality and ethics. Rationalism came to dominate social life as the spiritual receded.

A new judicial structure had to be erected to protect the gains of the rising class. Although medieval teaching had held that common ownership was more perfect than private, the new economic form stressed private ownership of productive property. New bodies of law were created as the scaffold around private property and economic activity; and the power of states was carefully redesigned not to threaten private interests but to conform to them. In the new system, "the principal function of the state," according to Fredrick Siebert, was "to maintain a stable framework within which the free forces of individualism may interact" (FT 53). We may take this to mean serving the general interests of private capital.

As economic, political, and judicial institutions were redefined, so was communications. One type of communication system had served religious and political needs but a new system began to develop out of commercial needs. Printing had been used early on as ideological support for the rising class and its arguments for individual liberty from control by state and religious authorities. A second phase began when printed matter became a commodity to be sold for recouping investment and generating profit. As the economic institution engulfed printing, the Copyright Act of 1709 in England and similar legislation in 1790 in the United States created private intellectual property and gave owners of this form the legal power to protect their economic interests and attack unauthorized users. A third phase developed later as owners of media commodified the very audience their products attracted and sold that audience to advertisers—what *Four Theories* calls "servicing the economic system." Humans no longer were just citizens or consumers; they became commodities that media owners produced. As capitalism ascended then, it embraced communications, an institution that heretofore had largely been immune to exchange value and the profit motive. In commodifying communications and redefining its premises, capitalism created its own New International Information Order.

Four Theories presents "the libertarian theory" as the ideological justification for the communications system capitalism developed, especially in the United States. If we view the development of liberalism as essentially a series of maneuvers by one class to fortify its rising position, however, we must ask whether this press theory was ever consciously expressed and whether it was perhaps nothing more than a self-serving rationale advanced by commercial interests.

The historical critique of liberalism is complemented by close readings of liberal theory. *Four Theories* identifies several writers and statesmen as builders of classical liberalism and the libertarian theory, especially John Milton, John Locke, and John Stuart Mill (FT 43–46), who are made to represent a much larger group of liberal writers and thinkers (for discussions of lesser known figures, see Levy 1985; Smith 1986; Keane 1991). While we do not want to reduce the works of the "great thinkers" to expressions of class interests, a closer look at these three reveals unexpected wrinkles in their relationships to the rising capitalist order.

Milton's *Areopagitica* ([1644] 1951) has already been discussed in chapter 2. We should note that this text has assumed almost biblical stature among those who see it as a foundation of the libertarian theory. Siebert hails it as "a majestic argument for intellectual freedom in the libertarian tradition" (FT 44). Steven Helle writes that "Milton advocates the derivation of truth from the free expression of all opinions, unrestrained by government endorsement or suppression of any position" (1982, 5). The columnist William Safire claims that *Areopagitica* "stands today as the greatest prose work in denunciation of censorship" (1975). Are these assessments accurate?

Rather than arguing for unlimited freedom of expression, Milton was calling for limited religious toleration and urging certain Protestant groups to stop warring among themselves so they could speed up "the slow-moving reformation which we labor under" ([1644] 1951, 53). Moreover, Milton did not advocate the end of state control of the press. On the contrary, he saw the useful role control could play in guarding and advancing the Reformation and argued for freedom from prepublication licensing only for Protestant men like himself. Nor was Milton arguing for the end of prepublication licensing of all material. He was clear about the limits of the liberty he was talking about, excluding Catholicism, open immorality, and anyone convicted of having "written and divulged erroneous things and scandalous to honest life" (33). He also looked down on the journalism of his day, which he did not bother to address in *Areopagitica,* and throughout 1651 was actually a licensor—that is, a censor—of newsbooks.

"Libertarian" is an irrelevant term for Milton. He was not arguing for broad liberty—"those neighboring differences, or rather indifferences, are what I speak of, whether in some point of doctrine or of discipline, which though they may be many, yet need not interrupt the unity of spirit, if we could but find among us the bond of peace" (52). Milton here seems to have the same concern for unity that Wilbur Schramm chidingly attributes to "Marx and his followers." They "have placed an almost mystical value on 'unity,'" Schramm writes, and have "displayed authoritarianism, fixedness, a tendency to make hard and sharp distinction between right and wrong, [and] an amazing confidence" (FT 107).

Something else overlooked by those who see Milton as the intellectual watershed of our communications system is a fundamental obstacle he found in the path of the search for Truth— the commercial motive. Milton believed the ultimate purpose of free expression was to find Truth, which he understood to be God's word. The Christian's duty, he was convinced, was to struggle to find that Truth. For Milton, this search was totally inconsistent with commercial aims. He lamented "the mercenary crew of false pretenders to learning" and applauded "the free and ingenuous sort of such as evidently were born to study and love learning for itself, not for lucre or any other end, but the service of God and of truth" ([1644] 1951, 29). By contrast-ing those who seek God and truth with the mercenary type motivated by money, Milton was restating the admonition in the Sermon on the Mount when Jesus taught "Ye cannot serve God and mammon." Milton was condemning the commercial motive in general as well as the licensing law that made no dis-tinction between "those whose published labors advance the good of mankind" and those with less lofty aims tainted by pe-cuniary gain.

The misidentification of Milton as a classical liberal is dou-bly misleading. Whatever we make of Milton's aims, it is folly to pretend, first, that he wanted all manner of opinions pub-lished and, second, that this is a characteristic of our media. Scholars of today who read Milton selectively not only do him a grave injustice but also mystify the nature of the contempo-rary communications system built on the pursuit of profit, which he patently abhorred. We must credit Milton with being quite honest about who he thought deserved to be heard, some-thing about which our media companies are much less explicit.

John Locke, who is said to be another contributor to the lib-ertarian theory, provided arguments in *Two Treatises on Civil Government* ([1690] 1940) for a representative state and private property. Basing his argument on natural rights and higher law, he wrote about consent as the basis for government but he meant the consent of those who hold the power to make deci-sions, not the consent of the governed (all people in society). Locke was hardly a democrat; he saw only a restricted group in society as holders of political power, and these people were the propertied classes. The state, Locke believed, was the product of a contract with the people, and it should exist only to pre-serve "lives, liberties, and fortunes" ([1690] 1940, 187). Since the majority did not have "fortunes" or property, Locke really was arguing for a class-based state that protected the haves from the have-nots. By contrast, four centuries earlier, Thomas Aquinas had argued that the poor, under stress of need, legitimately could steal from the rich ([1265–71] 1947, 1480–81). Less than seventy years after *Two Treatises,* Jean-Jacques Rousseau implicitly argued against Locke in an essay inquiring into *The Origin of Inequality among Men* (1754). Rousseau asserted that wealth purchases power and privilege and creates political institutions that protect the propertied classes at the expense of others. Inequality produces ignorance that prevents the oppressed from recognizing their actual situation and from understanding that civil laws ratify property relations in society. Instead, Rousseau declared, the knowledge the oppressed can acquire is irrelevant to their real needs.

With his theory of private property, Locke tried to explain how "men might come to have property" even though God had given the world "to mankind in common." Locke declared that private property is created when a person labors, mixes his human essence with something, and removes it from the state of nature. "Labour . . . makes it his property . . . [and] no man but he can have a right to [it]." But Locke added a small qualifier with monumental consequences: "The turfs my servant has cut . . . become my property without the assignation or consent of anybody" ([1690] 1940, 130). Surely the turf would belong to the servant if Locke's initial principle were followed. Rather, it is the purchase or ownership of another's labor power that allows the buyer to claim property. Labor indeed creates value and property, as Locke contended, but often for somebody other than the laborer; it is this value and property, Locke argued, that the state should protect.

Locke limited the amount of land and its fruits a person could properly own: as much as one could use before it spoiled—more than that was an offense against God and the common good. No such limitation applied to money, however. Locke, then, was providing a justification for the rising commercial, merchant, and manufacturing classes that accumulated the capital necessary for the takeoff of industrial capitalism. Using the labor of others to reproduce and multiply capital was not improper,

Locke argued, and neither was using state power to protect capital and preserve the property system. That it was right was obvious to any reasonable, thinking citizen.

Locke was hardly arguing for the broad interests of humanity. He was arguing on behalf of a class that stood to benefit from the liberty it sought for itself. No wonder Locke was popular with many revolutionaries in the colonies who constructed a state form that excluded the bulk of the population from the political process. As a deist, he provided the justifications for secularizing economic conduct and in so doing reversed traditional Christian concerns about money and stewardship. Locke legitimized the unlimited seeking of wealth, spurred the rise of possessive individualism, and provided the explanation for why some people are poor—they are not industrious.

John Stuart Mill's *On Liberty* ([1859] 1979) is cited as another landmark in the formation of the libertarian theory. (Yet his essay on basically the same subject, "The Spirit of the Age" [(1831) 1965], in which he comes to different conclusions, is overlooked. Mill pointed out in his *Autobiography* that drafting *On Liberty* was a "joint production" with his wife, Harriet, and that "the whole mode of thinking" in the book "was emphatically hers" [(1873) 1969, 149, 150] though this collaboration is ignored in most commentary, including *Four Theories*.) *On Liberty* deals with "the nature and limits of the power which can be legitimately exercised by society over the individual" ([1859] 1979, 59) and not with the liberty of mass communications. The libertarian theory, however, makes no distinction between the two. Libertarians argue that the corporation is a legal person and must have the same rights as a biological person, though the former has greater resources and more social, economic, and political power.

As a fastidious intellectual, Mill was concerned that the democratization of society was incompatible with individual distinction, and he deplored the leveling he saw around him: "Formerly, different ranks, different neighbourhoods, different trades

and professions lived in what might be called different worlds.
. . . They now read the same things, listen to the same things,
see the same things, [and] have their hopes and fears directed
to the same objects" ([1859] 1979, 139), as if Mill were talking
about the impact of today's media. With the expansion of the
electorate and the "ascendancy of public opinion in the State,"
Mill believed, "there ceases to be any social support for non-
conformity" (140). He elevated individuality in the way previous generations of liberals had lauded the individual. Mill
wanted a society in which people were left alone to pursue their
own tastes and interests, so long as no one harmed others. Happy individuals make a happy society. He saw tyranny of the
majority, not tyranny of the state, as the central problem—how
to restrain other people from imposing their standards on intelligent individuals. The value of "those who stand on the higher eminences of thought" is that they provide "the counterpoise
and corrective" to "the opinions of masses of merely average
men" (132).

Like Locke, Mill was not much of a democrat. In fact, in
Thoughts on Parliamentary Reform, published the same year as
On Liberty, Mill strongly advocated a system of plurality of votes
in which individuals of "superior knowledge and cultivation"
should be given more votes than the "ordinary unskilled labour-
er" (1859, 25–26). While Locke had provided arguments for popular government, Mill felt himself the victim of "public opinion [that] now rules the world" ([1859] 1979, 131). To him, public
opinion was just the voice of "masses," "that is to say, collective
mediocrity. . . . The mass do not take their opinions from dig-
nitaries in Church or State, from ostensible leaders, or from
books. Their thinking is done for them by men much like themselves, addressing them or speaking in their name, on the spur
of the moment, through the newspapers." Mill lamented "the
present low state of the human mind" and that democracy could
never rise above mediocrity (131).

In numerous ways, Mill attacked what *Four Theories* claims

to be the linchpins of the libertarian theory. For example, he questioned "the dictum that truth always triumphs. . . . It is a piece of idle sentimentality that truth, merely as truth, has any inherent power denied to error" ([1859] 1979, 89, 90). He also was skeptical that there were objective truths awaiting discovery by rational humans. "Truth . . . is so much a question of the reconciling and combining of opposites that very few have minds sufficiently capacious and impartial to make the adjustment with an approach to correctness" (110). But Mill did argue that, at least in politics, it was necessary for "all the . . . antagonisms of practical life [to be] expressed with equal freedom and enforced and defended with equal talent and energy," otherwise there is no chance that each will receive adequate hearing. (Equal treatment for clashing points of view is hardly provided by today's media. As just one example, did the eight presidential candidates on the Illinois ballot in 1992 receive even approximately equal coverage in news media?)

While much of Mill's writing seems to be at variance with what the propounders of the libertarian theory report, Mill did provide one intellectual justification that would become important in contemporary society. In his indifference to ultimate philosophical questions, Mill relegated natural rights and God's will to the background and in so doing rejected metaphsyical grounds for ethical, moral, and religious standards. Extreme self-interest justified by utilitarian considerations took their place. "The only freedom which deserves the name is that of pursuing our own good in our own way" ([1859] 1979, 72), and it was the task of government and other institutions to promote that individual freedom. The ultimate test of whether an action was right or responsible was whether it pleased the individual. Though Mill argued (in *On Utilitarianism* [(1836) 1962]) against the simplistic hedonism of the first generation of utilitarians, his political writings provide no obstacle to the sort of self-seeking behavior encouraged by consumerism and advertising. Coincidentally, Mill simply took for granted that the press should be privately owned, since there was no point in adding unwarranted powers to the state, especially because, he contended, individuals can do things better. Mill understood, though, that a privately owned press was not necessarily synonymous with a profit-driven press, and more than two decades before publishing *On Liberty* he lamented that "newspapers are a mere investment of capital for the sake of mercantile profit" ([1836] 1962, 70).

So the liberal thinkers are an odd crew: Milton is no liberal; Milton, Locke, and Mill no democrats—and Mill is deeply suspicious of both the people and the mass circulation press. The contribution of these thinkers to the modern press system seems less an endorsement of free expression than an acceptance of property rights.

What is true of these thinkers is just as true of the practical documents of liberalism, especially the U.S. Constitution. It was created in secrecy by representatives of the propertied classes, not the broad population. The Constitution was a carefully wrought document that limited democracy and political participation, while state laws established property qualifications for voting and holding office (Parenti 1990, 143). As James Madison argued in *The Federalist,* the task of the Constitution and the republic it creates is "to preserve the spirit and the form of popular government" without much of the substance and to attenuate "factions" whose "most common . . . source" has been the "unequal distribution of property" (Hamilton, Jay, and Madison [1787–88] 1960, 58, 56). Liberalism, built we are told by believers in equality and freedom, delivered those cherished qualities to a minority, the propertied classes, as Locke and Adam Smith said it should.

The First Amendment should be understood in this context. Like the Constitution as a whole, the First Amendment reaffirmed laissez-faire and an antipathy to the state, while enshrining the libertarian concept of negative freedom. The Amendment identified five kinds of expression of conscience—religion, speech, press, assembly, and petition—and barred Congress from interfering with them. It was a noble sentiment, especially for the press, which was becoming more and more a part of the business system.

Commentators have said that the First Amendment guarantees, among other things, a free press and a free flow of information. (Would this mean that countries without a First Amendment, such as Canada, do not have a "free" press?) Granting that the Amendment prohibits Congress from abridging freedom of speech, does it thereby guarantee an unobstructed flow of ideas and information as well as a press free from any restraint? Of course not. The Amendment only says Congress cannot prohibit you from expressing yourself, if you want and if you have the means. It does not say that people with something to say will be able to say it, and it does not provide for the means to do so. Theordore Peterson concedes that "although free expression is a universal right, the citizen cannot claim the right to reach the audience of any of the mass media. He [*sic*] cannot demand, as a right, that a newspaper or radio station transmit what he says" (FT 97). Siebert claims that "the most persistent problem facing democratic societies is determining proper limitations to freedom of expression in the mass media" (FT 53). To the contrary, the most persistent problem is how to open things up and achieve a vibrant diversity of viewpoints.

Neoliberalism has supplemented the "negative" liberty of the First Amendment with "positive" liberties such as the right to know. The derivation of the public's right to know from the First Amendment is murky. The right to know was advanced by Kent Cooper of the Associated Press in the 1940s. Whatever its provenance, the right to know as liberals understand it also fails to come to terms with inequalities in real rights. Thus, we might begin by asking, the right to know about what? Does the citizen have the right to know, for instance, about the internal policy-making processes of businesses? Does the public have the right to know about the financial conditions of the media companies that supposedly serve it? In short, does the public have the right to know how private capital manipulates its resources? Siebert tells us that "libertarian theory assumed that the government's business was the public's business" (FT 62), to which one must add: business's business is nobody's business. In this regard, the right to know gives not one ounce of power to the public. Perhaps the Freedom of Information Act should be extended to the private sector.

In considering the libertarian view of the First Amendment—that it guarantees freedom of expression—it is important to distinguish how it applies to citizens and to employees. The Amendment does protect the expression of the citizen (and the media owner) from state interference but it does not defend the working reporter's expression from control by the publisher or station owner and their surrogates. The shield of the First Amendment ends when the interest of property owners to control what they own and whom they employ begins. Siebert points out that "the first problem under any system of society is to determine who has the right to use the media" (FT 18). The answer is clear: the owners. Since the communications system is a profit-driven business, it cannot be free from this controlling imperative, and the First Amendment provides not the slightest protection from its influence.

Private capital virtually monopolizes media ownership in the United States. Can we talk of real competition in the flow of ideas and information (as liberalism contends) when one economic interest has almost exclusive control over that flow, defining its nature and using it for financial enrichment? Even what we understand as competition is narrowly constrained. We talk about outlets under different ownership but rarely about different forms of ownership. It is in the interest of media owners and their allies to protect this communications system and to have the state protect its general form by leaving it alone. The exception occurs when particular capital tries to use state power to shield itself from competition—as when newspaper publishing interests used the state to prevent telephone companies from entering the information creation and transmission business and when theater owners asked the state to encumber the growth of movie channels on cable television.

The self-interest of the media system extends to cultivating a favorable public image. Just as sellers of cars, hamburgers, and kitchen sinks seek to assure the buyer of the quality of their products, so media owners have the means to tell the consumer how fine their products are. Media, they say, operate free from interference in the marketplace and respond to public desires. Or as Schramm puts it, our media system "has 'just grown,'. . . grown according to the laws of public demand and private enterprise supply" (FT 130). This is liberalism's myth of the free press that it is in the interest of the press to perpetuate.

Alternatives to Capitalism

Any thoughts about alternative media systems must begin with the way *Four Theories* structures reality. As we pointed out earlier, the basic distinction in *Four Theories* is between "free" and "controlled" media systems. The "controlled" is exemplified by the Soviet communications system. The "free" is identified mainly with the U.S. system of privately capitalized, profit-driven newspaper publishing. This comes as no surprise. Since the libertarian theory is described in terms of U.S. newspaper publishing, which is founded on private capital and free from government control, then a capitalist press must be a free press.

Four Theories does not encourage thinking about "free" alternatives to capitalist media. The authors are not concerned with looking for variety or analyzing different ways of organizing media, even within Western capitalist countries. The dichotomy they set up leaves no room for explaining communications systems that are neither profit-motivated nor totalitarian. It leaves no room for examining alternatives outside the U.S. free and Soviet controlled polar opposites. We come away with the impression that, say, noncommercial educational broadcasting (as U.S. public broadcasting was called when *Four Theories* was published) is an aberration, excused as a supplement to real stations that are run as profit-driven businesses.

The alternative to the American-style press was the Soviet media system, and this is presented as the embodiment of Marxism. Schramm was ambivalent about Marx's actual contribution to this system, claiming at one point that Marx did not always approve what his followers were doing, yet declaring at another that the Soviet state is based on Marx's principles. Of course, Marx did not advocate state (or party) control of media (Guback and Bettig 1987), and he was equally firm about another matter: "the first freedom of the press consists in its not being a business" (Marx 1947, 61).

Unfortunately, then, *Four Theories* distorts, by ignoring them, media organized under rationales other than the Soviet or the private capital systems and fails to find a place for them in its typology. While this is not the place for lengthy discussion of this theme, examples of alternative media are available. The *Four Theories* template cannot explain the anticapitalist Christian press in the United States—publications that critique American capitalism from a Christian economic ethos.

In the nineteenth century, in what *Four Theories* must consider the heyday of the libertarian theory founded on private capital, newspapers were published by the Perfectionists, a Christian Protestant group in the eastern states that practiced community of property. They advocated "Bible Communism" and wrote of "true communism," which they understood to mean the community of believers cleansed in the blood of Christ (*Circular*, February 16 and March 2, 1853). Speaking of commercial newspapers in San Francisco, the *Circular* lamented that "seven altars have gone up to mammon, and probably not one to Jehovah" (August 20, 1853). In its issue of March 21, 1864, the *Circular* said: "Ever since we began to print, which was thirty years ago, about the time of the founding of the famous 'Penny Press,' we have had a scheme in our heads about the establishment of a 'Free Press.'" The Perfectionists were perfectly clear about what they meant by "free." They did not mean "without control," something that can never exist. They meant that their press was free from being an article of merchandise and consequently free to work for God's kingdom: "Jesus Christ taught men to make it their business to 'seek the kingdom of God and his righteousness' and to leave money-making to the heathen. But [Benjamin] Franklin, so-called Father of the American press, taught men to make money their business, and leave religion to women. And this nation has accepted the teaching of Franklin and rejected that of Jesus Christ" (*Circular,* September 21, 1853).

In our own time, the *Catholic Worker* newspaper proclaims that in capitalism, "the guiding principle is production for profit." Since "production determines need" and "because capitalism is maintained by class war," the Catholic Worker movement advocates a "complete rejection of the present social order and a non-violent revolution to establish an order more in accord with Christian values." "We believe in worker-ownership of the means of production and distribution, as distinguished from nationalization. This is to be accomplished by decentralized co-operatives and the elimination of a distinct employer class." The movement sees "universal ownership . . . as a stepping stone to a communism that will be in accord with the Christian teaching of detachment from material goods" (*Catholic Worker,* May 1972).

This is another press that does not try to delude itself, its journalists, or its readers, with claims of being free. Nor is objectivity proclaimed as a characteristic of its writing. Credit is due to this kind of alternative communications system and to others that speak with different voices for the honesty with which they announce what their principles are and where they stand.

Any discussion of alternative media systems must recognize two points. First, any such system has to be an alternative to something, and what that something is must be clear. Second, if we are talking about a democratic country, there must be popular participation in the planning, funding, and operation of those systems.

Identifying the object of an alternative is important because that act automatically highlights things that should be avoided and, consequently, things that should be goals. The media in the United States are almost exclusively owned and controlled by one economic interest—private capital. Private sector businesses are created to reproduce and multiply the capital of owners and lenders. If we brush aside the glossy rhetoric, profit is the ultimate product of business. It is not the by-product of good behavior in the marketplace. Since capital is mobile and knows no geographic boundaries, it flows to those sectors and areas that promise the greatest rewards commensurate with risk. The needs of media businesses to enrich owners, to provide lucrative salaries and benefits to high-level management, to repay principal with interest to lenders, and, in general, to support the business system constrain and channel the activities and goals of those media. The output of the media system is not just news, information, and entertainment, nor is it just the audiences who commercial media round up to sell to advertisers. Those are not the end-products. The ultimate product is profit. Milton was right to recognize that seeking such an end distorts what is accomplished.

Because private capital has a virtual monopoly and has cultivated audience expectations, there are few other standards against which to situate its performance, and this makes it difficult to envision alternatives. John Stuart Mill expressed it well: "If resistance waits till life is reduced nearly to one uniform type, all deviations from that type will come to be considered impious, immoral, even monstrous and contrary to nature. Mankind speedily become unable to conceive diversity when they have been for some time unaccustomed to see it" ([1859] 1979, 140).

The monopoly of private capital also means that the need for alternative and oppositional media forms has little chance of being given a hearing in conventional media or in the educational establishment. This, in itself, indicates the kind of closed media system that currently exists and belies the robust, open discussion that supposedly takes place. Media businesses and their trade associations also have effective public relations and lobbying arsenals to reinforce the status quo. What this comes down to is that the media system is so intricately a part of the corporate business system and so effectively supports it that any noticeable change in the media would have to embrace the general economic system as well.

An alternative agenda, therefore, must include stopping the erosion of the public sphere, which means containing the expansion of capital in areas of life previously shielded from it. As an example, there has been some effective action in halting the proliferation of Channel One throughout the public education system. Inroads obviously have been made but its control is far from total. Public bodies, too long on the defensive, too long reacting to the intrusions of capital, must look anew at how the public sphere can be reclaimed and rebuilt. But allies must be chosen carefully. The erosion has been encouraged by the very state that is supposed to represent the public interest but that too often settles for comforting the dominant classes. This is evident in the federal government's auction of electromagnetic spectrum space to users—a twentieth-century version of the privatization of the commons.

There can be no blueprint for how alternative media systems should be organized and operated because that would undercut the very democratic principles they are supposed to serve. Furthermore, no blueprint could possibly envision all the possible combinations for organization and operation that creative human minds could devise. Clearly though, and as a minimum, any alternative system must view people as citizens and coworkers, not as consumers with only economic value. The system must be opened up in many ways to encourage active participation of the public in creating content, managing and operating the system, and critiquing it. "Professionalism," a concept often used to shield media from the intrusion of popular participation, urgently needs rethinking. The present system thrives on passive media consumers who follow directions and advertisements.

Thinking about alternatives must be liberated from the belief that new technology, in itself, is necessarily a force for democracy or a force for solution of societal problems. Technology always is instrumentalized and does not have a life of its own apart from the institutions that innovate and use it. With tools of technology at their disposal, dominant institutions define solutions to problems as technical, scientific, and objective, rather than as moral, spiritual, or structural. An alternative media system is not necessarily one that offers three hundred, as opposed to fifty, cable channels or dozens of selective information services. They may be nothing more than a way to carve out, with surgical precision, particular audiences for sale to advertisers. Thinking about alternatives also must be liberated from the belief that information is replacing capital—a view implying that it is irrelevant how the means of communication are owned and for what purpose, a view that ultimately concludes that capital is irrelevant altogether.

We also must understand that what is at issue in thinking about alternatives is the control over social resources. We hear much talk about information highways for the computer age, highways that, we are told, will spur economic development and propel the country into the twenty-first century. Mammoth investments by the state are being called for. While the public is dazzled by the new technology and its benefits, much less attention is being given to who will own the system, who will decide how it is used, and for what purposes. There is little discussion, as well, about whether innovation of this new technology is worthwhile at all. If historical precedent is an indicator, it will be developed at public expense and given away by the state to private enterprise, as were space technology and communications satellites. An alternative policy is urgently called for.

In the same way, the Federal Communications Commission

(FCC) in 1992 outlined a plan for a fifteen-year transition to high-definition television (HDTV), at the end of which all current broadcast transmission and receiving equipment would be obsolete. Estimated replacement costs for broadcasters would be close to $20 billion and for consumers it would approach $68 billion. This commitment of enormous social resources for a new television transmission standard is being made on engineering and legalistic grounds with no attention to moral or ethical considerations. How such a sum of social wealth is used should be the subject of an intensive study that incorporates democratic policy-making procedures. In this case, an alternative media strategy must insist that technical change in itself is not change at all but instead fosters a perpetuation of control by already dominant parties and will not serve to ameliorate social ills.

The principles of stewardship and accountability to the public interest must be reaffirmed, particularly as they apply to communications systems. Lockean liberalism posits that the have-nots have no legitimate claim on the property of others. Translated to media terms, this means, as Peterson tells us, that a citizen "cannot demand, as a right, that a newspaper or radio station transmit what he [*sic*] says. . . . One's right to free expression must be balanced against the private rights of others" (FT 97), which would include the right of media owners to control their own property. The sanctity of private productive property, especially in a vital social area such as communications, urgently needs reconsideration. The greater the potential social impact of private power, the less that power retains its purely private character. The clichés of private property disguise its essentially public nature and provide the rationalizations that allow private power to pursue its own goals. Alternative media systems must accommodate the principle of individuals' entitlements, and such media systems must be held in trust for citizens.

5

The Changing Information Environment

❖ ❖ ❖

When *Four Theories* was written, many U.S. newspapers carried ads for segregated housing, it was still legal in a number of states for a husband to divorce his wife for being a bad housekeeper, and no one had ever seen what the earth looked like from outer space.

A lot has changed since the days when Elvis Presley could be an iconoclast. We touched on some of these changes earlier—the civil rights movement, the collapse of the Soviet Union, the rise of intelligent broadband digitized networks that carry television, film, telephone, and computer data at the same time. Of course these changes are momentous. Perhaps they are in fact epochal and will transform our notions of normative theory. Perhaps not—liberalism survived the industrial revolution, in spite of the challenge posed by Marxism and other leftist critiques. The industrial revolution so transformed Western societies that earlier languages of natural rights and the easy equation of liberty and equality seemed archaic, but a notion of a free and lively arena of public discussion remained the center of normative press theory. Liberalism became neoliberalism but remained liberal after all. Is there reason to think that current changes will produce a more fundamental shift?

One way to approach this question is to focus on the key terms of thinking about the press in the modern West. For our purposes, the most important terms are the nation-state, the public sphere, civil society, and the press. Since the eighteenth century, these concepts have structured liberal thinking about communications in a particular way. The most compelling analysis of this history has been offered by Jürgen Habermas ([1963] 1989; Calhoun 1992).

Habermas argued that a particular notion of the public sphere arose in eighteenth-century France, England, Germany, and the United States. The key driving force in this development was the rise of bourgeois capitalism. The economic changes associated with the rise of capitalism produced a particular configuration of "civil society," a term that has been used in many ways but that to Habermas includes the marketplace, religion, and domestic life—in other words, all of the areas of life that liberals sought to protect from state control. The great bourgeois revolutions of the eighteenth century then might be understood as building a wall of separation between government and civil society.

This split between state and civil society is often understood as a split between the private and the public. Private and public have meant many things to many people, of course, but in Habermas's analysis "private" means not just having to do with intimate things but also having to do with anything that involves a private or personal interest—hence his inclusion of economic life. Many people think of the marketplace as a public place and it is in some ways, but to Habermas, inasmuch as the marketplace is the place where individuals pursue self-interest, it is part of the private or of civil society. So where is public space?

Habermas argued that the public sphere is the space between civil society and the state. This space allows citizens to address the state but demands that they leave their individual interests behind when they do so. The citizen must frame all arguments in the public sphere according to two complementary rules:

personal negation and universal supervision. Negation means that the citizen must hide personal interests behind a veil, as it were—something similar to the concept of the veil of ignorance that John Rawls discussed (1971). Universal supervision means that we must assume that everyone in a society (actually or virtually) observes every action in the public sphere. With these rules in mind, eighteenth-century thinkers (e.g., Jefferson, discussed earlier) could assume that citizens were free and equal in public, even if they were altogether unequal in private—different in terms of wealth and status, age and religion, region and class. With private considerations hidden behind a veil and with the powerful under the virtual scrutiny of the entire citizenry, public discussion would necessarily be rational and public deliberations would necessarily be directed toward the common good.

The public sphere is a space only in a hypothetical sense, of course. You cannot point to a particular place and say, "There is the public sphere." But you can find places that give some concrete substance to the public sphere. To mention the most obvious, there are legislatures, elections, and assemblies of various sorts, all of which are considered legitimate only if they allow for universal access and do not discriminate on the basis of "private" matters. Then there are the media.

We tend to think of the media themselves as the public sphere. Conceptually, the media are not the public sphere, though at certain times in history they may have seemed like it. But at any time in modern history the media have been important places for public discussion and, even when they have not themselves constituted public forums, they have been important as sources of raw material for public discussion in other forums. In Western societies, the rules governing the public sphere have always been understood as rules for the media, too, though the relationship between the media and the public sphere has changed radically over time.

We can understand the changing relationship between the media and the public sphere by thinking about the different terms we use to describe the media. We might argue that different relationships are implied in the terms "the press," "journalism," and "the media." When the First Amendment to the U.S. Constitution was written, during the very coming-to-power of the bourgeois state, the media were thought of as "the press." In chapter 1, we argued that the press in this case was understood mainly as the printing press, not as the newspaper press, so that freedom of the press was thought of in the same terms as freedom of speech. The relationship of the media—that is, the press—to the public sphere was thus a very simple one: the press was a tool that citizens used to speak and some of this speech was public. The press was a good tool for that because, theoretically, any citizen had access to one, any citizen could make an argument that was anonymous (simply by using a pseudonym, a common practice at the time) and therefore meet the rule of negation, and any printed argument could be produced in such quantity that anyone could be thought to have access to it, thereby meeting the rule of universal supervision. None of these characteristics were entirely true, but they were true enough for practical purposes.

The press subsequently came to mean something else, that is the newspaper press. Rather than meaning the printing press, the term press came to refer collectively to newspapers and then to news media generally (and was often used as a plural—"the press are . . ."). This is still the prevalent meaning of the term, of course. The press in this sense has a different relationship to the public sphere. Rather than being the largely passive tool by which people communicate in public, it was supposed to function as a way of (actively) representing public discourse. In the nineteenth-century United States, the press did this mostly by amplifying the other arenas that embodied the public sphere—by printing verbatim speeches and debates from the legislature, relaying partisan information and exhortation to voters, and publishing legislation and judicial decisions. The nineteenth-century press was still dependent on other public bodies for both content and income—legislatures and parties produced the discourse and subsidized the newspapers in various ways. Partisan editors editorialized, of course, but did so generally as partisan functionaries and not as independent moral critics.

This press was not engaged in journalism as we understand the term. By journalism we generally mean the active collection and rendition into reports of matters of public interest. Journalism is something that reporters do, and reporters are creatures of the industrial revolution, part of the mass production of news that accompanied the industrialization of the newspaper. Journalism has a different relationship to the public and the public sphere than the press. Whereas citizens used the printing press to speak in public and the newspaper press spread the messages of the public organizations that sought to speak for citizens, journalists try to speak to citizens as if they, the journalists, were public information itself. Journalists, as we discussed in chapter 3, view themselves as expert public servants—though employed by private companies—and seek to acquire the autonomy and independence of professionals. Needless to say, the notion of freedom of the press changed when journalism colonized the press.

The industrial revolution also saw the creation of mass media besides the press. The end of the nineteenth and the beginning of the twentieth centuries in the United States and elsewhere witnessed the successful introduction of dime novels, mass circulation magazines, motion pictures, and radio. Some of these media might be called "the press" in the sense that they used printing presses, but others were not and were denied the rights granted the press in the First Amendment. Likewise, some of these media might be called public in the classic sense, but mostly they shunned the typical subject matter and etiquette of the public sphere.

Meanwhile, the citizenry was changing. Women and members of minority groups were enfranchised, and less privileged groups, often faced with crises of diminishing expectations and downward mobility, began to use politics—the one earthly arena where theoretically the poor and the rich were equal—to demand services from the government. These demands coincided with the demands of the middle and upper classes for benign institutions of social control (such as schools) to create what is called the bureaucratic welfare state, a development solidifed through the world wars and depression of the first half of the twentieth century.

These developments altered the traditional calculus of the public sphere. The distance between civil society and the state disappeared as the state became more and more involved in "the private"; the press became less a forum and more a source of news; the media, in contrast to the press, were less and less committed to the public sphere as classically conceived. All of these shifts are implied in the shift from classical liberalism to neoliberalism.

In the late twentieth century (and presumably in the early twenty-first) qualitatively different changes will pose new challenges to the normative concepts we associate with the public sphere. Journalism will change, just as the media and the state are changing and just as the public has changed. Already we have seen attacks on the bureaucratic welfare state, as well as challenges to state sovereignty by transnational corporations. Moreover, developments in media technology seem geared toward replacing broad audiences with increasingly narrow ones; the media that we have traditionally associated with universal audiences, including daily newspapers and network television, the dominant organs of journalism, are increasingly challenged. The public is represented less often by journalism and more often by polling. And the public sphere is more than ever permeated by the private.

At the horizon of current developments, we might stop talking about "the press" and "journalism" and "the media" and start talking about "information." The older terms, after all, seem to exclude many of the most interesting capacities of the new technologies, especially computers. They also exclude many of the more important features of older systems, including copyright and patent law. Shifting the term to information means, among other things, expanding the domain of law and regulation pertinent to communications theorists beyond the First Amendment (Braman 1988). At that point, the distinction between public and private will be entirely different from the "bourgeois" conceptions that Habermas has outlined and that have animated liberalism.

These developments are not confusing to Marxists. They amount to the erosion of the myths of bourgeois ideology in the face of the global development of capitalism. But to defenders of liberalism—whether neo- or classical—they seem like the end of the world as we know it. This is one story behind the panic about the decline of a common culture and of the liberal allergy to feminism, multiculturalism, and poststructuralism, all of which attack in theory the private/public distinction that has become so questionable in practice.

This chapter will examine current trends in light of these observations. We will begin with developments in the state, journalism, and the information infrastructure and conclude with a cursory look at some of the movements in thinking that have implications for normative theory.

Globalization and the Decline of the Nation-State

Four Theories made a series of assumptions that must be questioned. The authors assumed (1) that the nation-state determines the relationship between communications systems and the state, (2) that journalism plays the central role among communication media and genres in determining the relationship between the state and the policy, and (3) that the information/communication infrastructure is such that structural control over communicative practices is possible. Changes in the nature of the state, in the assignation of functions and roles within evolving communcations systems, and in the nature of the information infrastructure require each of these assumptions to be reexamined. We will begin with the nation-state.

Four historic trends contribute to the need to reconceptualize the state today. First, the form of the state that had dominated much of the developed world throughout most of the twentieth century—called the bureaucratic welfare state because it was characterized by the multiplication of federal agencies and a more extensive bureaucratic involvement in citizens' lives—began to be dismantled during the 1980s. This geopolitical change both resulted from and contributed to a questioning of the basic postulates of classical liberal thought. Second, the transformation of the information infrastructure and emergence of the "net"—the telecommunications network—as the dominant medium has led to a wide variety of frustrations for nation-states as they attempt to exercise traditional modes of power, such as control over either financial or information flows across their borders (the "vulnerabilities of the state"). Third, transnational corporations have come to rival and sometimes outweigh nation-states in the exercise of a variety of forms of power. Fourth, new conceptions of the state have become visible as a wide variety of states, including those of the newly industrialized countries, finds successful niches in today's global environment, as surviving concepts of the nation-state adapt to changed conditions and as new theories of the state are developed.

The press itself has become globalized. It is no longer only the nation-state out of which the press operates that most significantly determines journalistic practice. Globalization is evident in several dimensions.

The *subject matter* of journalism has become globalized. The social, political, economic, cultural, and ecological phenomena and processes that are the subject matter of journalism are no longer bound by national borders. Significant decision-making processes that affect domestic affairs take place now in the international arena or within private sector transnational corporations that are for many purposes locationless in nature. The actors about whom journalists report, therefore, are now global. Events of journalistic significance—environmental degradation, war, economic trends—have global, not local, impact.

Similarly, the *constituency* of journalism has become globalized. The "constituency" of journalists for *Four Theories* was the "citizenry" of individual and discrete nation-states. The citizenry, however, are also members of "civil society," that is, society as it has interests separate from (and sometimes against) those of the state. In much of the world this concept is newly of interest as societies struggle to conceptualize and organize themselves under shifting geopolitical conditions. Speaking of civil society emphasizes people's relationships with each other as their primary civic identity, as opposed to their relationship with the state indicated in the concept of citizenship.

Once the state is removed as the primary lens for civic identity, global influences upon identity in today's environment become more visible. We are beginning to see more and more expressions of a sense of being members of a global civil society, sharing concerns as much with those beyond nation-state borders as with those within. "Nongovernmental organization" (NGO) is the legal designation for organizations that represent global interests of civil society vis-à-vis nation-states and international organizations. The number of these and their relative influence in international and national decision-making arenas is growing.

Recognition of environmental problems has been a particular stimulus to discussion of shared global concerns. Another influence has been the increasing globalization of governmental surveillance systems, in which citizens and noncitizens alike are subjects of surveillance. In a third important area of activity that quite self-consciously has stimulated a sense of shared global concerns, the emergence of "new security theory" aims to generate a sense of a shared security blanket East and West. And last, of course, shared cultural elements—Coca Cola, jeans, and Madonna—have created global age cohorts on the cultural front.

News *institutions* are intimately intertwined in the global processes that are driving industries generally toward oligopolies comprised of larger and larger transnational corporations—fewer and fewer news organizations now provide information to the world. The result is a demonstrable reduction in the diversity and number of news sources available through the mass media. We expect this trend to increase.

Along with the globalization of news organizations, those elements that comprise the sociology of journalism, journalistic *procedure,* have also become globalized. Thus the "beat," or geographically defined terrain of a reporter's domain for coverage (the courthouse, Washington, Latin America), has become global. What Gaye Tuchman called the "bureaucratic phase structure" (1978), or the time-defined terrain of a reporter's domain for coverage (decisions of the U.S. Supreme Court, the passing of a budget by Congress, etc., all refer to pegging news to the passing of stages of procedures internal to other institutions), has also become globalized with the globalization of significant actors. As the number of news organizations communicating news globally has declined, the role of the gatekeeper or editor within each surviving news organization takes on a global character (e.g., editors at CNN).

Regulation of communication practices is also increasingly moving to the international arena, following the globalization of the infrastructure and of the social interactions associated with communications. Thus, decisions of the ITU, UNESCO, GATT, World Intellectual Property Organization (WIPO), and other organizations have as much to do with determining the environment within which journalists operate as does the nation-state.

The Decline of the Press

Liberal theory supposed an intimate relationship between the nation-state, the national public, and the press. By the middle of the twentieth century, the press was thought to play a role in the development of the nation-state in four ways:

- The press provided the primary conduit for information flows between the government and the people.
- The press provided a public space in which members of civil society could discuss matters of public concern.
- The press served as the arbiter of facticity and therefore as the site for debates over facticity.
- It was through the press that the emerging nation-state could find its rhetorical expression.

[handwritten margin note: all these literal roles are challenged]

Today's media environment challenges each of these roles.

The press was supposed to be an information conduit adequate to fulfill all of the basic functions of a communications system required for a functioning democracy. Governmental and legal matters are still published in newspapers as a matter of official—often law-required—policy. Less formally, the *New York Times* still claims to present all relevant news of U.S. politics, though it now contends with CNN for national and global agenda-setting. More indirectly, politicians and others use journalists in a variety of ways to communicate with the public and with each other.

Just as the press was supposed to represent the government to the people, so was it supposed to represent the people to the government. Editorials and opinion pages in print and public access broadcasting in radio and television are considered important ways for the public to communicate with the government. Public opinion polls are often both conducted by and reported in the press.

These roles have been systematically critiqued. Sociologists describe ways in which the mutual interdependence between reporters and sources—and thus between the institutions of journalism and those of government—systematically constrain the types of information that will actually flow through journalism as a conduit, and the ways in which it is shaped (Ericson, Baranek, and Chan 1989; Tuchman 1978). In the other direction, it is obvious that communications from the public to the government via the press are so few as to be meaningless in all but the most elite publications. Public opinion polls, too, are no longer considered neutral conduits (Herbst 1993). The press only partially and largely unidirectionally fulfills the role of information conduit between government and citizens.

Thinking of the press as a conduit seems to run counter to the tradition of journalism. One motif in communications law that treats the press as a conduit is "neutral reportage." This doctrine emerged within libel law to protect the news media when they reported on negative comments made in public settings; as long as it had merely served as a "neutral conduit" in disseminating the comment, the medium itself was protected from libel charges. As the doctrine has developed, however, it has become a means by which the courts can specifically dictate reporting and editing procedures; down this path the journalist becomes a mere piece of production equipment with no independent intelligence and judgment.

Other types of information conduits between government and citizens are now available. These conduits are charged with transmitting three categories of information: (1) information the dissemination of which is promoted by the government (discussed above), (2) information about the government, and (3) information the creation of which is demanded or promoted by the government. Each of these presents its own problems and patterns.

Information disseminated by the government proliferated throughout the past century. The growth of the bureaucratic welfare state multiplied the number of conduits for information flows from the government to citizens. Governments send information they choose through media such as school systems, rural extension services, and health systems.

It is worth noting that the U.S. government has *not* seen public broadcasting as a medium through which the elements of a shared national culture might be communicated. While this perspective allegedly derives from a commitment—hard fought—not to permit the government to shape the content of public television and radio, in more than a few other societies public television has been understood to play a role much like that of public education and so came under heavy government control. In Western Europe, discussion about continuing the commitment to a shared national culture via broadcasting and determining just what that culture should be (should it include minorities? should it represent only "high" culture?) dominates debates as their systems become deregulated and governmental involvement becomes more negotiable, at times negligible. In all societies this is an important issue as channels for information multiply and audiences fragment.

Information about the government is one area in which fables about new information technologies might become real. Within the United States, dozens of counties and municipalities have already put governmental information on-line with provisions for interactivity with citizens through a variety of means, including facilitating conversations of citizens with each other on matters of governmental concern. An early goal of the Clinton/Gore administration was to bring the federal government if not exactly "on-line" at least accessible via electronic mail. The possibilities are alluring. A recent trial in Santa Monica, California, showed that public libraries' provision of free access to on-line services such as these did in fact extend participation in governmental affairs to socioeconomic classes for whom access is not otherwise available. Not only did the homeless and others—most of whom had access to computerized data bases and electronic mail for the first time through the libraries—participate in public discussions on matters concerning their affairs but they were also able to use services accessed electronically to otherwise empower themselves and improve their personal situations.

It does seem possible—*logistically,* at least—to use the information infrastructure to extend democratic participation in and knowledge of governmental affairs and in the process to further empower individual citizens. Logistical solutions do not, however, touch the problems of *political will* that continue to color and often impede efforts to extend democratization through this means, as we mentioned in chapter 3. A genuine commitment to do so requires universal access in every dimension—educational, technological, logistical, economic, and cultural. Simply giving citizens access to government information will not automatically empower them in civil society. In a world where transnational corporations operate beyond the reach of the nation-state, other kinds of access or empowerment are clearly called for.

There have already been radical shifts in the communications environment, and these shifts have meant changes in law and regulation. Ithiel de Sola Pool (1983) has warned that we might lose significant freedoms as the law adapts to new technologies. While classical liberalism emerged in an environment dominated by print, we now live within a global electronic network. Some features of the emerging information infrastructure are especially salient to policy makers (Braman 1993).

First, the infrastructure is now truly ubiquitous globally. Individual travelers have always carried information from place to place, and the electronic network has been genuinely international since its beginnings with the telegraph in the middle of the nineteenth century (Headrick 1990), but we are now experiencing the qualitatively different process of globalization (Featherstone 1990; Robertson 1992). In a globalized environment, our policy making must consider additional actors besides "the government" and "citizens," as well as relationships with other systems (nation-states, organizations, and societies) and their constituencies.

Second, the infrastructure is far more highly articulated, with intelligent nodes in the hands of individual users. The kinds of control against which communications policy was constructed are changing and, in many cases, no longer pertinent. Federal efforts to control encryption programs, for example, are useless against free distribution of such programs via the net. Habitual focusing on obsolete forms of control can distract from identifying and pursuing actual forms of control in the electronic environment.

Thus, for example, specific protection of the right to *process information* appears to have become necessary. It is striking to note that while the FCC was going through the tortures of the *Computer Inquiries,* in which the agency attempted to distinguish between "basic" and "enhanced" information transmission for the purposes of distinguishing between the telecommunciations services that would remain regulated and those that would not, the courts were dealing with the question of whether or not the government should be permitted to prevent (via prior restraint, which is anathema in the United States) the magazine *The Progressive* from publishing plans for how to build a hydrogen bomb. Here the government's argument was directed against the *processing* of information. While it was not denied that all of the information from which the author drew was in the public domain, it *was* claimed that processing that information—thinking about it, in other words—was not permitted! That is, while the government could not restrict access to information in the public domain, it attempted to justify restricting speech by forbidding the processing of information leading up to that speech.

These two examples show the limits of traditional First Amendment law in the new environment. In the *Computer Inquiries,* the FCC sought to distinguish between types of information processing for the purposes of differential regulation; in the *Progressive* case the government sought to restrict communicative rights by forbidding information processing. In neither case was First Amendment analysis prepared to deal with attacks on communicative rights that used the tactic of defining them as other, more easily regulable types of activities or by distinguishing between stages of an information production chain for the purposes of differential legal or regulatory treatment.[1]

Third, the capacity of the infrastructure has become vast, virtually nullifying scarcity as a grounds for regulation of communications institutions, facilities, and processes. Any restrictions on information creation, processing, flows, and use must be based on other grounds. Scarcity was extremely important in the justification of broadcasting regulation in the United States, for much of that regulation runs counter to consensually accepted interpretations of the First Amendment (Douglas 1987; Horwitz 1991; McChesney 1993).

Fourth, the emerging system is "geodesic" and "fractal." Rather than a few channels going to mass audiences, use of the net connects an indefinite number of points with each other in ways that permit multiple routes. Peter Huber (1987), addressing the U.S. Department of Justice as it struggled with yet more consequences of the divestiture of AT&T, identified the fractal nature of the infrastructure as significant for communications policy because it meant that decisions about whether or not to centralize or decentralize control over communications need no longer be made once for the entire system but could be made over and over again as they involved particular types of communications in specific locales in ever-repeating fractal patterns of complexity.

Fifth, this environment is turbulent, at times chaotic, and much of its turbulent nature is a consequence of the use of new information technologies. Complexity, turbulence, and chaos are both problematic characteristics of the environment with which policy must deal and potential effects of policies being considered. Any model of a communications system that drives policy must be dynamic, not static, in order to accommodate chaos within its conceptual terms.

Just how the emerging communications environment will affect the flow of information about the government to the people will depend on other factors. In the United States, under Bill Clinton and Al Gore, we are currently undergoing an enormous change of position on this point. The Ronald Reagan and

George Bush administrations clearly distinguished two classes of informational citizens: those within government, who have the right to know, and those outside of government, who have the right to know only what those in government think they should know. This led to a policy that, whether dealing with the Freedom of Information Act, the information classification system, or with office management systems within federal agencies, sought to restrict access to governmental information. In many cases, the Reagan and Bush administrations were able to utilize legislation that actually came into effect under Jimmy Carter, as with the notorious Paperwork Reduction Act that so empowered the Office of Management and Budget (OMB) to dictate federal agency practices and as in other areas of communications policy, such as the deregulatory strand. Clearly, Clinton and Gore are committed to reversing this policy.

It remains to be seen whether this overall policy shift will enhance the government's role in explaining complicated policies and procedures to affected citizens. It is also yet to be seen if the Clinton and Gore focus on information policy will reach this area of the law, a First Amendment issue from the point of view of those who argue that the First Amendment includes, among other things, a right to receive information. This leads to the next type of information flow between governments and people: information creation mandated/sponsored by the government.

National governments are involved in a variety of types of information creation. Constitutional provisions mandating government collection of information include most often and importantly those calling for a census but also, occasionally, provisions that call for government collection of information about some element of the natural environment (the weather, ocean, atmosphere). A number of national governments are also given constitutional authority to collect information about financial matters, anything related to taxation, and for a variety of other purposes. As elaborated by the bureaucratic welfare state, these powers are increasingly contestable and contested in the 1990s.

Support for research and development is another area of governmental information that is growing in importance but generally generated by statutory, not constitutional law. Through a variety of tools that outline and support industrial policy, governments directly and indirectly sponsor and encourage research of particular kinds. The results of this work can be considered governmental information in two ways. It is government-*triggered* information—information that in many cases may not have come into being without government direction and funding. It is also, as a consequence of funding involvement, government-*owned* information, for in the United States the federal government has property rights in the results of any research toward which it contributed support.

Issues involving governmental property rights in this type of information will become more important as intellectual property rights move to the center of the legal battleground over access to resources. The debate over encryption provides a vivid current example. The U.S. government has long recognized the importance of encrypting information for business purposes; as the electronic storage and transmission of such information has become more common, the need for encryption has grown. Yet at the same time, the government feels a need to be able to eavesdrop on electronic information flows. In the early 1990s, the irony of the government's position became obvious when it moved to prevent the marketing of encryption systems that would make it impossible to "wiretap" transmissions and instead proposed to make its own system, the "Clipper chip," mandatory. The effects of government-triggered information are experienced by us all as the information moves out of the "research" phase and into the "development" of products.

So the new information environment promises significant changes in information flows from governments to people. What about the other direction? There were always alternatives to the press as conduits for the thoughts of citizens to flow to the government. Direct petition and the right to call for referenda frequently appear as constitutional provisions. Federal support for a national information infrastructure—a postal system—is generally justified by the need to ensure that representatives of the people can communicate with their constituents in a two-way process.

The bureaucratic welfare state multiplied, often through regulatory or administrative law, the means of communication with the government for citizens, though the rules are generally directed toward narrow categories of speech on particular issues. It is a fundamental assumption of most notions of procedure that there must be a means through which the individual can communicate with the decision-making body.

Enthusiasts expect much more from new technologies. Ross Perot has repopularized an old element of the utopian notion of the information society as one in which, via what some have called "teledemocracy," we are able to do away with representative government and bring everything to a vote before the people. With today's technologies, this presumably would mean "educating" the public about issues via television and then taking a national plebiscite, as can be done even with touch-tone phones. Research, however, has shown that those whose primary source of news is print are able to articulate arguments for their positions on issues and choices of candidates, while those whose primary source of news is broadcast may have positions and candidates but will not be able to articulate why. And as James Carey (1989) has pointed out, in the notion of participatory democracy that drove early U.S. history, the town hall discussion significantly included the community talking an issue over among its citizens before voting, not just the act of voting. This kind of discussion is not possible electronically and not, therefore, even possible as a part of what is idealistically termed "teledemocracy," for a significant element of the democratic process, the conversation, is not there.

Group discussion via radio and television talk shows cannot substitute, nor can computerized bulletin board virtual communities, for each of these is "thin" in terms of the range of social interactions with which they are engaged. Each will be focused on a particular issue that may be explored in depth by a group of people who either come together by chance or whose personal interests lead them to pursue a particular set of issues—but who have no other necessary connections with each other.

This is important because it is precisely the characteristic of a community that it must live with itself—that disagreements aired in the town hall in a political discussion one day must be lived with in the local marketplace, on the docks, or in the coffeehouse the next day. It is this need to live with each other in the thickness, the richness of the multiple types of human interactions that historically led to the notion of *civitas,* of the civilization centered on the city. Multiplication of interactions revolving around particular needs or interests might satisfy those specific needs or interests—but it might not contribute to the formation of the whole necessary for the self as well as for the community. And it clearly will not replace community-wide discussion about public issues in what is still romantically referred to as the public sphere.

In discussions about the nature of journalism and its role vis-à-vis civil society, the notion of the public sphere has come to dominate discussions in Western, Central, and Eastern Europe and the former Soviet Union (Dahlgren and Sparks 1991). In the previous section, when communication was characterized as information flows, we inevitably emphasized what James Carey (1989) has called the transmission model of communication. To focus on the public sphere is to deal with a "ritual" model of communication in which the "product" is not a message or a commodity but a community.

The concept of the public sphere is often criticized for being very difficult to operationalize—just where *is* the public sphere? Colin Sparks and Anna Reading (1993) argue that there is no civil society in some of the Central and Eastern European countries or in the former Soviet Union—and therefore the notion of the public sphere loses its content. Karol Jakubowicz (1990) identifies three different public spheres in Poland as that state began to reformulate itself. Bruce Robbins and his colleagues (1993) argue that the public sphere is altogether phantom in an electronic environment.

One of the most common ways of operationalizing the concept is to think of the press as the public sphere. While this is conceptually incorrect, there have been times and places when the multitude of daily newspapers represented an active public discussion among quite distinct perspectives, so that it operated like a simulacrum of the public sphere. This is not true of most places today. In an environment in which there are fewer and fewer media voices out of larger and larger conglomerates (it is the irony of CNN's ubiquitous global success that in the United States, at least, we now have less diversity of sources about international news than ever before) the press no longer provides anything like a public sphere.

Electronic bulletin boards are a closer fit. Often anonymous, generally inexpensive to access, often appealing to those who are otherwise marginal socially, they are providing a new venue for public discussion the particular characteristics of which are not yet well understood. It has already been demonstrated, however, that local elections can be won by campaigns run only via electronic bulletin boards and that alternative political groups can find their global organizing tasks greatly facilitated by using electronic mail through networks such as PeaceNet and EcoNet.

Traditional mechanisms for public discussion survive, of course. Assembly and public speech are often used by citizens as a means of addressing the government. Marches, demonstrations, and riots are all efforts to give voice in such a manner that it will be heard by those in power.

Still, the question of where there is really room for public discussion outside the confines of the state, unconstrained by conditions established by the nation-state, is difficult to answer. While electronic communication provides a new venue, it is not accessible to all, nor is it likely to be a venue in which discussions are conducted in privacy—that is, without surveillance by the government and other parties whose activities may well be the very subject of the discussions being watched. Journalism clearly does not provide a genuine public sphere in any meaningful sense of the term. As tensions heighten within universities and colleges, higher education less and less provides a venue for open discussion. At times it seems as if, while the number of *channels* of communication may have multiplied and our capacity grown vastly, the amount of actual communication taking place has decreased.

So far we have dealt with two of the traditional roles of the press in terms of the changing information environment. We have argued that, despite their limitations, new media are replacing the press as conduits for information flows from governments to people and from people to governments. In similar fashion, the press is losing its privileged role as a definer of facticity.

Several hundred years ago, fact and fiction became distinguished out of the undifferentiated narrative matrix of the medieval period (Davis 1983). The press's role was on the front lines, so to speak, of facticity—the first ones to collect the "facts" to be subsequently sifted through by historians and analysts of various kinds. The sense of being involved in a factual enterprise fundamentally distinct from fictions of any sort has been central to the journalist's identity in modern liberal societies. It is also a presupposition of the notion of objectivity. For this reason, attacks upon the integrity of "objective journalism" from the 1960s on were particularly painful to those who saw their role as soldiers in the war to build meaning, find history, identify the stuff about which our stories would be told.

Attacks on objectivity have come from several sources. Studies of the sociology of journalistic processes and institutions demonstrate the ways in which selective collection, perception, and transmission of facts shape stories to parallel the worldview of dominant institutions. Meanwhile, literary theory has emphasized the fictive aspects of every kind of text, including "nonfiction" such as history and news. In a rebellion that took note of these scholarly criticisms, "New Journalists" argued that a truer story is told by admitting human biases and reporting what one actually sees as an individual, not as dictated by major institutions. While the two approaches to journalism—"old" and "new"—retain a dichotomy, in practice over the last few decades journalists in both camps have come to share each others' practices as required by specific stories or encouraged by specific institutional resources or needs.

This "blurring of genre" (Geertz 1983) is of course not unique to the practice of journalism but is one of the characteristics of the postmodern condition. By now the claim to facticity of all narratives has been questioned at the most profound level. Self-reflexivity has come to be the first requirement for the legitimacy of a text. Questioning the role of journalism as the definer of facticity thus echoes more general analyses of social trends and developments of social theory. Today, we can all but visibly see institutions competing with each other as definers of facticity, using a variety of communicative means, but among them journalism no longer appears to play the decisive role. Indeed, the credibility of journalists relative to other definers of fact appears to be in a sliding decline.

The one historic role that the press continues to play in ways most like traditional forms is as a rhetorical site for the nation-state. The press has always been a place in which the key symbols and rhetorical devices that drive the nation-state have been worked through. Since Reagan, American presidents have learned to appeal to the public via the mass media without going through the institutional gatekeepers that have historically controlled the news—via cable television, often using satellite transmission, or videotape. Still, the mainstream news media continue to play a role in our political life.

The press no longer performs the same functions in the same ways that it did when *Four Theories* was conceived. As a conduit of information the press is overwhelmed by contending services. As a model public sphere it is said to exist no longer. As a definer of facticity it is on the decline, and the notion of facticity itself is quite diminished. The press has retained some of its role as a voice of the nation-state, but that voice itself is now often confused and to listeners is only one voice among many. In sum, the press can no longer be identified as uniquely important to the functioning of a democracy.

The Changing Relationship between the Press and the State

Classical liberalism—tightly linked to the development of the nation-state—assumed a focal and necessary interdependence between the press and the nation-state. Freedom of the press is justified because it serves the governmental form (democracy) of the nation-state; it is the job of the press in essence to serve as an additional arm of the government, a "fourth estate," and to play the role of "watchdog" of the nation-state; governmental requirements for communicating with the public specify publication in newspapers as well as posting in public places. The assumptions are that the nation-state is the primary concern of the press and that the constraints on communications activities are most likely to come from the nation-state.

The emerging environment challenges this traditional relationship. With the decline of the nation-state and the rise of extra-governmental actors (largely transnational corporations) often equal to or greater than nation-states in their resources and power, the linkage between the press and the nation-state no longer seems so integral to the definition of the role of the press relative to civil society. It is likely that this process will continue to accelerate.

In this environment, concerns about communicative rights must be as attentive to threats from the private sector as they classically have been to threats from governments. Policy makers must correspondingly expand their conceptualization of the forms of power with which declarations, laws, and regulations are concerned. Concerns about the right to communicate must deal with contraints that may come from factors such as the hegemonic force of the spread of specific types of organizational forms as carried out by transnational corporate actors, as well as more traditional restraints upon communicative rights exercised by the state. (One of the great weaknesses of First Amendment law, for example, is that it is directed only toward state action—actions on the part of the government—and therefore has decreasing relevance in our privatizing environment.)

A similar expansion is appropriate in the global context. Unfortunately, all of the significant international arenas that have historically influenced communications policy are under attack: UNESCO is riven over budgetary and ideological matters; the ITU has become ever more politicized over the past decade, threatening its continued effectiveness; and international trade mechanisms are increasingly troubled. While there is talk of replacing these arenas with new ones, new legal developments are occurring primarily in contract law, beyond the gaze of both policy makers and the public.

The novel problems of the emerging information environment provide additional justification for detailing the communicative rights to be specifically protected. For example, since freedom to process information is under threat, there is reason to specify it as a right. So ought we also to protect the other stages of the information production chain. Such rights are implied by but not specified in traditional protections of the right to free expression.

Public and Private

Whatever the changing information infrastructure brings, we can expect continuing modifications in the demarcation between private and public. It is characteristic of late twentieth-century Western societies that public and private have become more intertwined, because of both the continuing penetration of both the state and even more dramatically the marketplace into the "intimate" sphere, and also because of the countervailing pressing of "intimate" issues into the realm of politics. These trends are most visible in issues regarding gender and are most forcefully analyzed by feminists.

Feminists are, of course, a diverse group, covering a wide social, political, and intellectual spectrum. In simple terms, this diversity is usually resolved into a dichotomy between liberal and radical feminists. This dichotomy serves well in discussing positions regarding the public/private split.

Liberal feminists embrace liberal individualism. They focus on issues of procedural equality (equality under the law) and equal rights, arguing that the goal of feminism is to eliminate gender discrimination. Liberal feminists preserve the public/private split. They do criticize the historical fact that the public sphere well into the twentieth century was gendered male—women could not vote and were expected to devote themselves to domestic matters. To liberals, however, the gender bias of the public sphere can be redressed without demolishing the whole construct.

To radical feminists, such hopes are naive. In fact, they argue, the concept of the bourgeois public sphere depends in its origins and its persistence on male domination (Benhabib 1987; Fraser 1992; Pateman 1989). Male equality in public is based on male dominance in private; men can be civic equals only because they are domestic sovereigns. So it is not accidental that the line between public and private corresponds so exactly to the line between the traditionally male and the traditionally female. In fact, this opportune designation is one of the chief devices of patriarchy.

There is no question that seventeenth- and eighteenth-century liberal thinkers—Locke, Rousseau, Jefferson—excluded women. It went without saying that the dictum "all men are created equal" applied only to males; women who tried to remedy this flaw in liberal theory, such as Mary Wollstonecraft, were generally ignored. But isn't the problem solved by just counting in women?

Radical feminists argue, on the contrary, that this only makes the exclusion more elusive. Eliminating gender bias in the public realm is only cosmetic, because inequality in the private realm persists. Since women's oppression, unlike that of racial and ethnic minorities, occurs most tellingly in the intimate sphere, then the apparatus that declares intimate matters unsuitable for public discussion will necessarily reinforce this oppression.

Liberal feminists counter by emphasizing the historical importance of procedural rights. Just as a wall of separation protects religion from the state, so should a veil be drawn over gender and sexuality. Groups that have successfully achieved acceptance and empowerment have done so by claiming their rights as individuals and consigning their group characteristics— skin color, language, income—to the realm of the private, the place where religion had already gone. This means that no person's domestic situation (e.g., single motherhood) can be used to discriminate; it does not mean that the interests of single mothers cannot be addressed in public. It is as fair for a woman to promote women's interests in public as it is for a factory-owner to promote manufacturers' interests or a farmer to promote agricultural interests.

The disagreement between liberal and radical feminism enters into the realm of media and communications most notably in the area of pornography. To one group of radical feminists, best exemplified by Catharine MacKinnon (1993), pornography is the penultimate expression of male domination. Pornography presents male domination in intimate settings in such a way as to make it seem natural; in doing so, it silences women, who simply will not be heard if they must share a stage with *Deep Throat*. MacKinnon therefore rejects arguments against regulating pornography on the basis of the right to privacy. The pretense that pornography is of only private concern ignores its main function, which is to continually reinforce patriarchy and disempower women.

The workings of pornography are mystified by appeals to freedom of expression, MacKinnon argues. Pornography is not really about expression—it is about power. And unlike expression, which is usually thought of as unlimitedly shareable, power is a zero-sum game. One person or group can have power only at the expense of another person or group.

Conclusion

Here we might broaden the discussion again. There is a persistent notion that the emerging "information society" will be different from previous societies because its chief resource (information) is infinitely renewable: it is not depleted by its consumption; it can be used without being used up. This is true only in the abstract. In concrete situations, information acquires its value not from being shared but from being treated like any other commodity—being used by its owner to guarantee profit. The "information society" is a big, bright cliché, and it is easy to see why people are attracted to it, but the hopes reposed in it are doomed to be disappointed. The information society will not eliminate informational inequalities unless some way is found to overcome preexisting social inequalities—whether based on money or race or sex. Information in its present configuration (like pornography?) is about power, not expression.

Note

1. The fact that First Amendment analysis has not yet coped with these two problems does not mean that distinctions between stages of the information production chain aren't already significant to a number of areas of information law, defined broadly as that law which pertains to any stage of the information production chain. A study of all such decisions by the U.S. Supreme Court from 1980 to 1986 revealed a great, albeit unconscious, sensitivity to distinctions between types of information processing and stages of an information production chain (Braman 1988).

Conclusion

[handwritten: normative theory maps]

This book has addressed an instance, embodied in *Four Theories of the Press,* of a particular tendency in normative theory. This is the tendency to map. *Four Theories* presented a durable but now questionable map of normative press theory. Is it time to draw another map?

If mapping is possible, the authors of this book probably are not the group to do it. We come from a diverse set of disciplines—law, ethics, history, journalism, advertising, political economics, and communications theory—and hold a diverse set of beliefs—Marxism, libertarianism, liberal democracy, radical democracy, and communitarianism. This range of disciplines and positions does not easily map onto a schema of normative press theories and certainly not that of *Four Theories.* Does this mean that we recommend abandoning hope in ever drawing a more adequate map?

In chapter 1, we made two sorts of arguments against the *Four Theories* schema. One was that *Four Theories* had asked the wrong constitutive questions. Choosing to constitute theories around answers to the questions of the nature of "man," the state or society, knowledge, and truth necessarily led to a schema that pivoted on liberal terms. Indeed, in our detailed criticisms of the theories, we argued that the libertarian theory and its nicer younger sibling, social responsibility theory, were presented sympathetically and with historical concreteness, while the authoritarian theory and the Soviet communist theory were essentially straw men and bogeymen.

[handwritten right margin: schema liberal-biased]

[handwritten right margin: authoritarian and Soviet theories → straw men]

This criticism implies that a more adequate schema could be constructed by asking more adequate constitutive questions. Some of these questions are urgently being pressed in current debates: What is the relationship between economic structures and political movements? Do groups have rights or do only individuals have rights? Is freedom of expression about truth or about power? Where should the line between public and private be drawn? Surely any normative press theory will have to answer these questions; surely we could think of others equally pertinent.

But the *Four Theories* project assumed that a set of answers to its constitutive questions would form a coherent theory. It assumed that a finite number of fundamental questions could determine a complete range of thought, much as Euclid tells us that three points determine a plane. That's where our second sort of criticism comes into play.

Our second critique was that the theories actually mentioned were driven not by ideas but by history. That is to say that much of what *Four Theories* presents as the reasoned elucidation of clear answers to fundamental questions was really ex post facto rationalization of pretty accidental developments. Given the proper circumstances, we might argue, any "libertarian" might be an authoritarian (witness the later Milton, a minor functionary in a military dictatorship) and any authoritarian might be a libertarian (witness Plato's adulation of the gadfly Socrates). In other words, we doubt that any number of constitutive questions—no matter how carefully chosen—will produce a tight fit between the answers and social policy.

This second critique advises us to do history and not theory. It advises us to treat normative theories as ideologies and not as ideas, as historically specific cultural formations and not as generalizable moral precepts. But we are not satisfied with that.

Walter Benjamin has presented an unforgettable metaphor for historical understanding:

[margin handwriting: theories not idea-driven, but by history]

A [Paul] Klee painting named "Angelus Novus" shows an angel looking as though he is about to move away from something he is fixedly contemplating. His eyes are staring, his mouth is open, his wings are spread. This is how one pictures the angel of history. His face is turned toward the past. Where we perceive a chain of events, he sees one single catastrophe which keeps piling wreckage upon wreckage and hurls it in front of his feet. The angel would like to stay, awaken the dead, and make whole what has been smashed. But a storm is blowing from Paradise; it has got caught in his wings with such violence that the angel can no longer close them. This storm irresistibly propels him into the future to which his back is turned, while the pile of debris before him grows skyward. This storm is what we call progress. (Benjamin 1968, 258–59)

Benjamin's angel of history is full of good intentions but, needless to say, helpless, despite his omniscience. He cannot cure the past, he cannot halt the passage of time, and perhaps worst of all he cannot turn around to face the future.

Like the angel of history, we are full of good intentions. We all believe in some version of democracy, some notion of freedom, and some role that the media can play in achieving these. But we believe in wildly different notions of democracy and freedom. We can understand our differences by stringing them together as a historical narrative or by spreading them out as social or political differences, but this makes it difficult for us to face forward and negotiate these differences as if they were (what they might in fact be) differences in ideas.

In this book we rarely have transcended the historical mode. Primarily we have situated matters in their historical context and critiqued the way others have understood them. To someone who really admires *Four Theories,* our book probably reads like an account of Benjamin's catastrophe, piling wreckage upon wreckage.

We would like to do something else. In fact, most of us have in other works where we have argued for a particular normative position as paramount. Here we are concerned not with a single position, however, but with an entire terrain.

Four Theories has a nobility that our book lacks. It nobly believed that it could combine an essentially historical enterprise with an abstract schema of normative theories. Its belief, though, relied on its (covert) use of liberal premises for its constitutive questions. It seemed to succeed in mapping *all* the normative theories because it mapped them from just one.

None of us, as individual authors, is without such a map. But we acknowledge our maps are constructed *within* a normative paradigm. Obviously, a communitarian's map will not match a libertarian's. And the disparities between these maps matter a great deal: where one lists Australia, the other has the simple legend, "There be dragons here."

So perhaps a new map will come only when a new moral consensus is achieved. Or perhaps another group of scholars will figure out some better way. Or perhaps we have outlived the age of maps—maybe what we really need is a dictionary or a phone book.

Works Cited

Agnew, Spiro. 1969. Address to the Midwest Regional Republican Committee at Des Moines, Iowa, Nov. 13. Reprinted in *New York Times,* Nov. 14, p. 24.

Bacon, Francis. [1620] 1955. *Novum Organum.* In *Selected Writings,* ed. Hugh G. Dick. New York: Modern Library.

Bagdikian, Ben H. 1990. *The Media Monopoly.* 3d ed. Boston: Beacon Press.

Baker, C. Edwin. 1994. *Advertising and a Democratic Press.* Princeton, N.J.: Princeton University Press.

Barron, Jerome. 1973. *Freedom of the Press for Whom? The Right of Access to the Mass Media.* Bloomington: Indiana University Press.

Barton, Bruce. 1927. "The Creed of a Modern Advertising Man." *Printer's Ink,* Nov. 3, p. 3.

Benhabib, Seyla, ed. 1987. *Feminism as Critique.* Minneapolis: University of Minnesota Press.

Benjamin, Walter. 1968. *Illuminations.* New York: Schocken Books.

Berlin, Isaiah. [1958] 1969. "Two Concepts of Liberty." Pp. 118–72 in *Four Essays on Liberty.* New York: Oxford University Press.

Blanchard, Margaret. 1977. "The Hutchins Commission, the Press, and the Responsibility Concept." *Journalism Monographs* 49.

Blasi, Vincent. 1981. "Toward a Theory of Prior Restraint: The Central Linkage." *Minnesota Law Review* 66, no. 11: 70–82.

Bollinger, Lee C. 1991. *Images of a Free Press.* Chicago: University of Chicago Press.

Boorstin, Daniel G. 1974. "Advertising and American Civilization." Pp. 11–23 in *Advertising and Society,* ed. Yale Brozen. New York: New York University Press.

Braden, Maria. 1992. "*Ms.* Doesn't Miss the Ads." *Quill* 80 (Jan.–Feb.): 25.

Braman, Sandra. 1988. "Information Policy and the United States Supreme Court." Ph.D. dissertation, University of Minnesota.

———. 1993. "Global Surveillance, Media Politics, and Civil Liberty." *Media Development* 40, no. 2: 36–40.

Calhoun, Craig, ed. 1992. *Habermas and the Public Sphere.* Cambridge: MIT Press.

Carey, James. 1989. *Communication and Culture: Essays on Media and Society.* Boston: Unwin Hyman.

Chafee, Zechariah, Jr. 1941. *Free Speech in the United States.* Cambridge: Harvard University Press.

———. [1947] 1965. *Government and Mass Communications.* Chicago: University of Chicago Press.

Christians, Clifford, and Mark Fackler. 1980. "Liberty within the Bounds of Virtue: With Special Reference to John Milton's Political Prose." Pp. 16–41 in *Ethics and Mass Communication,* ed. Anne van der Meiden. Utrecht, Netherlands: State University of Utrecht.

Christians, Clifford, John P. Ferre, and Mark Fackler. 1993. *Good News: Social Ethics and the Press.* New York: Oxford University Press.

Clark, Charles S. 1991. "Advertising under Attack." *CQ Researcher,* Sept. 13.

Collins, Ronald K. L. 1992. *Dictating Content.* Washington, D.C.: Center for the Study of Commercialism.

Commission on Freedom of the Press (Hutchins Commission). 1947. *A Free and Responsible Press.* Chicago: University of Chicago Press.

Dahlgren, Peter, and Colin Sparks. 1991. *Communication and Citizenship: Journalism and the Public Sphere in the New Media Age.* New York: Routledge.

Danzing, Fred. 1992. "Drug Marketers Confront Study Authors." *Advertising Age* 63 (Jan. 27): 46.

Davis, Lennard. 1983. *Factual Fictions: The Origins of the English Novel.* New York: Columbia University Press.

Dewey, John. 1939. *Freedom and Culture.* Buffalo: Prometheus Books.

Douglas, Susan. 1987. *Inventing American Broadcasting, 1899–1922.* Baltimore: Johns Hopkins University Press.

Dworkin, Ronald. 1977. *Taking Rights Seriously.* Cambridge: Harvard University Press.

Emerson, Thomas I. 1977. *The System of Freedom of Expression.* New York: Random House.

Ericson, Richard V., Patricia M. Baranek, and B. L. Chan. 1989. *Negotiating Control: A Study of News Sources.* Toronto: University of Toronto Press.

Fackler, P. Mark. 1992. "Debates in Contemporary Theory: Richard Rorty and Charles Taylor." Paper presented at the National Conference on Communication Ethics, Gull Lake, Michigan.

Featherstone, Mike. 1990. *Global Culture: Nationalism, Globalization, and Modernity.* London: Sage.

Fox, Stephen. 1985. *The Mirror Makers.* New York: Vintage.

Fraser, Nancy. 1992. "Rethinking the Public Sphere: A Contribution to the Critique of Actually Existing Democracy." Pp. 109–42 in *Habermas and the Public Sphere,* ed. Craig Calhoun. Cambridge: MIT Press.

Geertz, Clifford. 1983. *Local Knowledge: Further Essays in Interpretive Anthropology.* New York: Basic Books.

Glasser, Theodore, and James Ettema. 1993. "When the Facts Don't Speak for Themselves: A Study of the Use of Irony in Daily Journalism." *Critical Studies in Mass Communication* 10, no. 4: 322–38.

Gossage, Howard Luck. 1987. *Is There Any Hope for Advertising?* Urbana: University of Illinois Press.

Graber, Mark A. 1991. *Transforming Free Speech: The Ambiguous Legacy of Civil Libertarianism.* Berkeley: University of California Press.

Guback, Thomas, and Ronald Bettig. 1987. "Translating the *Manifesto* into English: Nineteenth-Century Communication, Twentieth-Century Confusion." *Journal of Communication Inquiry* 11, no. 2: 3–16.

Gutmann, Amy. 1985. "Communitarian Critics of Liberalism." *Philosophy and Public Affairs* 14 (Summer): 308–22.

Habermas, Jürgen. [1963] 1989. *Structural Transformation of the Public Sphere.* Cambridge: MIT Press.

Hamilton, Alexander, John Jay, and James Madison. [1787–88] 1960. *The Federalist.* New York: Random House/Modern Library.

Hay, George (Hortensius). [1799] 1970. *An Essay on the Liberty of the Press.* New York: Arno Press.

Haydon, Graham. 1978. "On Being Responsible." *Philosophical Quarterly* 28:46–51.

Hayek, Friedrich A. von. 1944. *The Road to Serfdom.* Chicago: University of Chicago Press.

———. 1973–79. *Law, Legislation and Liberty: A New Statement of the Liberal Principles of Justice and Political Economy.* 3 vols. Chicago: University of Chicago Press.

Headrick, Daniel. 1990. *The Invisible Weapon: Telecommunications and International Politics, 1851–1945.* New York: Oxford University Press.

Helle, Steven J. 1982. "The News-Gathering/Publication Dichotomy and Government Expression." *Duke Law Journal* 32:1–60.

Herbst, Susan. 1993. *Numbered Voices: How Opinion Polling Has Shaped American Politics.* Chicago: University of Chicago Press.

Hill, Christopher. 1972. *The World Turned Upside Down: Radical Ideas during the English Revolution.* London: Maurice Temple Smith.

———. 1977. *Milton and the English Revolution.* New York: Viking Press.

Hocking, William E. 1912. *The Meaning of God in Human Experience.* New Haven: Yale University Press.

———. 1918. *Human Nature and Its Reworking.* New Haven: Yale University Press.

———. 1947. *Freedom of the Press: A Framework of Principle.* Chicago: University of Chicago Press.

———. 1964. "Interrogation of Martin Buber." *Philosophical Interrogations* 1 (Oct.).

Horwitz, Robert. 1991. *The Irony of Regulatory Reform.* New York: Oxford University Press.

Huber, Peter. 1987. *The Geodesic Network: 1987 Report on Competition in the Telephone Industry.* Washington, D.C.: U.S. Department of Justice, Antitrust Division.

Illo, John. 1972. "The Misreading of Milton." Pp. 178–91 in *Radical Perspectives in the Arts,* ed. Lee Baxandall. Harmondsworth: Penguin.

———. 1988. "Areopagiticas Mythic and Real." *Prose Studies* 11, no. 1: 3–23.

Jakubowicz, Karol. 1990. "Musical Chairs? The Three Public Spheres of Poland." *Media, Culture, and Society* 12:195–212.

Jefferson, Thomas. [1787a] 1950–. To Edward Carrington, Paris, Jan. 16. In *The Papers of Thomas Jefferson,* ed. Julian P. Boyd et al. 21 vols. Princeton, N.J.: Princeton University Press. 11:49 (hereafter cited as *Papers*).

———. [1787b] 1950. To William Carmichael, Paris, Dec. 15. In *Papers,* 12:423–27.

———. [1787c] 1950. To James Madison, Paris, Dec. 20. In *Papers,* 12:438–43.

———. [1798] 1903. "Kentucky Resolutions." In *The Writings of Thomas Jefferson,* ed. Andrew Lipscomb. 20 vols. Washington, D.C.: Thomas Jefferson Memorial Association. 17:379–91 (hereafter cited as *Writings*).

———. [1803] 1903. To Mr. Pictet, Washington, D.C., Dec. 5. In *Writings,* 10:357.

———. [1804] 1903. To Abigail Adams, Monticello, Sept. 11. In *Writings,* 11:49–52.

———. [1807] 1903. To Thomas Seymour, Washington, D.C., Feb. 11. In *Writings,* 11:154–56.

———. [1811] 1903. To James Monroe, Monticello, May 5. In *Writings,* 13:59.

———. [1814] 1903. To Dr. Walter Jones, Monticello, Jan. 2. In *Writings,* 14:46.

Jensen, Jay. 1957. "Liberalism, Democracy, and the Mass Media." Ph.D. dissertation, University of Illinois at Urbana-Champaign.

Karp, Walter. 1983. "The Lie of TV's Political Power." *Channels of Communication* 3 (May–June): 37–40.

Keane, John. 1991. *The Media and Democracy.* Cambridge: Polity Press.

Leiss, William, Stephen Kline, and Sut Jhally. 1986. *Social Communication in Advertising.* New York: Methuen.

Levin, Gary. 1992. "Seagram Runs Selective Ads." *Advertising Age* 63 (Jan. 27): 44.

Levy, Leonard. 1960. *Legacy of Suppression: Freedom of Speech and Press in the United States.* Cambridge: Harvard University Press.

———. 1963. *Jefferson and Civil Liberties: The Darker Side.* Cambridge: Harvard University Press.

———. 1985. *Emergence of a Free Press.* New York: Oxford University Press.

Locke, John. [1690] 1940. *Two Treatises on Civil Government.* London: J. M. Dent and Sons.

MacIntyre, Alasdair. 1981. *After Virtue: A Study in Moral Theory.* Notre Dame, Ind.: Notre Dame University Press.

MacKinnon, Catharine. 1993. *Only Words.* Cambridge: Harvard University Press.

Madison, James. [1787] 1941. "Madison's Report on the Virginia Resolutions." In *The Debates in the Several State Conventions on the Adoption of the Federal Constitution.* 2d rev. ed. Ed. Jonathan Elliot. 5 vols. Philadelphia, Pa.: J. B. Lippincott. 4:570–71.

Mannheim, Karl. 1936. *Ideology and Utopia: An Introduction to the Sociology of Knowledge.* New York: Harcourt Brace.

Marx, Karl. 1947. *Marx and Engels on Literature and Art,* ed. and trans. Lee Baxandall and Stefan Morawski. New York: International Publishers.

Matsuda, Mari. 1993. *Words That Wound: Critical Race Theory, Assaultive Speech, and the First Amendment.* Boulder, Colo.: Westview Press.

McChesney, Robert. 1993. *Telecommunications, Mass Media, and Democracy: The Battle for Control of U.S. Broadcasting, 1928–1935.* New York: Oxford University Press.

McIntyre, Jerilyn S. 1987. "Repositioning a Landmark: The Hutchins Commission and Freedom of the Press." *Critical Studies in Mass Communication* 4:136–60.

Meiklejohn, Alexander. 1948. *Free Speech and Its Relation to Self-government.* New York: Harper and Brothers.

Mill, John Stuart. [1831] 1965. "The Spirit of the Age." Pp. 3–35 in *Mill's Essays on Literature and Society,* ed. J. B. Schneewind. New York: Collier.

———. [1836] 1962. *On Utilitarianism.* New York: Modern Library.

———. 1859. *Thoughts on Parliamentary Reform.* London: John W. Parker and Son.

———. [1859] 1979. *On Liberty.* New York: Penguin Books.

———. 1867. "Inaugural Address at the University of St. Andrews." *Dissertations and Abstracts.* Vol. 4. Boston: Spencer.

———. [1873] 1969. *Autobiography,* ed. Jack Stillinger. Boston: Houghton Mifflin Company.

———. 1962. *Essays on Politics and Culture,* ed. Gertrude Himmelfarb. New York: Doubleday and Co.

Milton, John. [1644] 1951. *Areopagitica and Of Education.* Arlington Heights, Ill.: Harlan Davidson.

Mumford, Lewis. 1934. *Technics and Civilization.* New York: Harcourt Brace.

Nozick, Robert. 1974. *Anarchy, State and Utopia.* Oxford: Basil Blackwell.

———. 1993. *The Nature of Rationality.* Princeton, N.J.: Princeton University Press.

Orwell, George. 1949. *1984.* New York: New American Library.

O'Toole, John. 1992. "Battle on to Save Drug Ads." *Advertising Age* 63 (Oct. 26): 24.

Parenti, Michael. 1990. "The Constitution as an Elitist Document." In *The United States Constitution,* ed. Bertell Ollman and Jonathan Birnbaum. New York: New York University Press.

Pateman, Carole. 1989. *The Disorder of Women: Democracy, Feminism, and Political Theory.* Stanford, Calif.: Stanford University Press.

Patterson, Orlando. 1991. *Freedom.* Vol. 1: *Freedom in the Making of Western Culture.* New York: Basic Books.

Pool, Ithiel de Sola. 1983. *Technologies of Freedom.* Cambridge: Harvard University Press.

Pound, Roscoe. 1911. "The Scope and Purpose of Sociological Jurisprudence." *Harvard Law Review* 25:140–43.

———. 1915. "Interests of Personalty." *Harvard Law Review* 28:343–453.

Ragan, Fred D. 1971. "Justice Oliver Wendell Holmes, Jr., Zechariah Chafee, Jr., and the Clear and Present Danger Test for Free Speech: The First Year, 1919." *Journal of American History* 58:24–45.

Rawls, John. 1971. *A Theory of Justice.* Cambridge: Harvard University Press.

———. 1985. "Justice as Fairness: Political not Metaphysical." *Philosophy and Public Affairs* 14:223–51.

Robbins, Bruce, ed. 1993. *The Phantom Public Sphere.* Minneapolis: University of Minnesota Press.

Robertson, Roland. 1992. *Globalization: Social Theory and Global Culture.* London: Sage.

Rorty, Richard. 1979. *Philosophy and the Mirror of Nature.* Princeton, N.J.: Princeton University Press.

———. 1988. "The Priority of Democracy to Philosophy." Pp. 257–82 in *The Virginia Statute for Religious Freedom,* ed. Merrill D. Peterson and Robert C. Vaughn. New York: Cambridge University Press.

———. 1989. *Contingency, Irony, and Solidarity.* New York: Cambridge University Press.

Rousseau, Jean-Jacques. [1754] 1992. *The Origin of Inequality among Men,* ed. Roger D. Masters. Trans. Judith R. Bush. Hanover, N.H.: University Press of New England.

Safire, William. 1975. "Ghost of Locke." *Champaign-Urbana Courier,* Jan. 21 (New York Times News Service).

Sandel, Michael J. 1982. *Liberalism and the Limits of Justice.* Cambridge: Cambridge University Press.

Schmidt, Benno, Jr. 1976. *Freedom of the Press v. Public Access.* New York: Praeger.

Schramm, Wilbur, ed. 1948. *Communications in Modern Society.* Urbana: University of Illinois Press.

———, ed. 1949. *Mass Communications.* Urbana: University of Illinois Press.

———. [1951] 1973. *The Reds Take a City.* Westport, Conn.: Greenwood Press.

———, ed. 1954. *The Process and Effects of Mass Communications.* Urbana: University of Illinois Press.

Schultze, Quentin. 1982. "'An Honorable Place': The Quest for Professional Advertising Education, 1900–1917." *Business History Review* 56 (Spring): 16–32.

Siebert, Fredrick Seaton. 1952. *Freedom of the Press in England, 1476–1776.* Urbana: University of Illinois Press.

———. 1953. "The Historical Pattern of Press Freedom: Functions and Control of the Mass Media." *Vital Speeches* 19 (Aug. 15): 659–62.

Smith, Donald. 1986. *Zechariah Chafee, Jr., Defender of Liberty and Law.* Cambridge: Harvard University Press.

Smith, Jeffery A. 1988. *Printers and Press Freedom: The Ideology of Early American Journalism.* New York: Oxford University Press.

Sparks, Colin, and Anna Reading. 1993. "Broadcasting and Civil

Society in Eastern Europe." Paper presented to the International Association for Mass Communication Research, Dublin, Ireland.

Taylor, Charles. 1989. *Sources of the Self: The Making of the Modern Identity.* Cambridge: Harvard University Press.

————. 1991. *The Ethics of Authenticity.* Cambridge: Harvard University Press.

Thomas Aquinas. [1265–71] 1947. *Summa Theologica.* New York: Benziger Brothers.

Tillich, Paul. 1954. *Love, Power and Justice.* New York: Oxford University Press.

Tuchman, Gaye. 1978. *Making News: A Study in the Construction of Reality.* New York: Free Press.

Unger, Roberto Mangabeira. 1976. *Law in Modern Society.* New York: Free Press.

Walzer, Michael. 1983. *Spheres of Justice.* New York: Basic Books.

Waters, Harry F. 1992. "On Kid TV, Ploys R Us." *Newsweek,* Nov. 30, p. 88.

Wigdor, David. 1974. *Roscoe Pound: Philosopher of Law.* Westport, Conn.: Greenwood Press.

Woodward, Wayne. 1993. "Toward a Normative-Contextualist Theory of Technology." *Critical Studies in Mass Communication* 10, no. 2: 162–73.

Wortman, Tunis. 1800. *Treatise concerning Political Enquiry, and the Liberty of the Press.* New York: G. Forman.

Wyatt, Robert O. 1991. *Free Expression and the American Public.* Murfreesboro: Middle Tennessee State University Press.

Authors

WILLIAM E. BERRY is an associate professor in the College of Communications and the director of the media studies program at the University of Illinois at Urbana-Champaign. His publications deal with minority issues and the telecommunications industry, and he is the author of the forthcoming *Magazine Journalism: Theories, Strategies, Practice.*

SANDRA BRAMAN is an assistant professor in the Institute of Communications Research at the University of Illinois at Urbana-Champaign. She is the author of numerous articles on policy, the telecommunications net, and the information society, and of *The Information Regime: The Common Use of Information Policy Tools in International Trade, Defense, and Agriculture* (forthcoming).

CLIFFORD CHRISTIANS is a professor in and the director of the Institute of Communications Research at the University of Illinois at Urbana-Champaign. He is the coauthor, with William Rivers and Wilbur Schramm, of *Responsibility in Mass Communications* (3d ed., 1980); with Kim Rotzoll and Mark Fackler, of *Media Ethics: Cases and Moral Reasoning* (3d ed., 1991); and with John Ferre and Mark Fackler, of *Good News: Social Ethics and the Press* (1993).

THOMAS G. GUBACK is a professor in the Institute of Communications Research at the University of Illinois at Urbana-Champaign. His publications include *Counterclockwise: Perspectives on Communication by Dallas Smythe* (1994) and *The Communications Industry in the American Economy* (forthcoming).

STEVEN J. HELLE is a professor in and the head of the Department of Journalism at the University of Illinois at Urbana-Champaign.

He is the author of numerous articles on media law, including most recently "Whither the Public's Right (Not) to Know? Milton, Malls, and Multicultural Speech" (*University of Illinois Law Review*, 1991).

LOUIS W. LIEBOVICH is an associate professor in the Department of Journalism at the University of Illinois at Urbana-Champaign. His publications include *The Press and the Origins of the Cold War, 1944–1947* (1988) and *Bylines in Despair: Herbert Hoover, the Great Depression, and the News Media* (1994).

JOHN C. NERONE is an associate professor in the Institute of Communications Research at the University of Illinois at Urbana-Champaign. His publications include *The Culture of the Press in the Early Republic: Cincinnati, 1793–1848* (1989) and *Violence against the Press: Policing the Public Sphere in U.S. History* (1994).

KIM B. ROTZOLL is a professor in and the dean of the College of Communications at the University of Illinois at Urbana-Champaign. He is the coauthor, with James Haefner and Charles Sandage, of *Advertising in Contemporary Society* (4th ed., 1995); with Charles Sandage and Vernon Fryburger, of *Advertising Theory and Practice* (12th ed., 1989); and with Clifford Christians and Mark Fackler, of *Media Ethics: Cases in Moral Reasoning* (4th ed., 1995).

Index